everyday Phonics

Intervention Activities

Table of Contents

Using Everyday Phonics Intervention Activities

Current research identifies phonemic awareness and phonics as the essential skills for reading success.

- **Phonemic awareness** is the ability to notice, think about, and work with the individual sounds in spoken words. Before children learn to read print, they need to become aware of how the sounds in words work. They must understand that words are made up of speech sounds, or phonemes.

- **Phonics** instruction teaches children the relationships between the letters (graphemes) of written language and the individual sounds (phonemes) of spoken language. Children learn to use the relationships to read and write words. Knowing the relationships will help children recognize familiar words accurately and automatically, and "decode" new words.

Although some students master these skills easily during regular classroom instruction, many others need additional re-teaching opportunities to master these essential skills. The Everyday Phonics Intervention Activities series provides easy-to-use, five-day intervention units for Grades K–5. These units are structured around a research-based Model-Guide-Practice-Apply approach. You can use these activities in a variety of intervention models, including Response to Intervention (RTI).

Getting Started

In just five simple steps, Everyday Phonics Intervention Activities provides everything you need to identify students' phonetic needs and to provide targeted intervention.

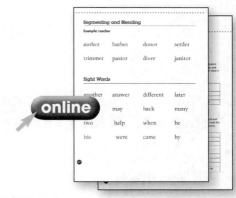

1. PRE-ASSESS to identify students' Phonemic Awareness and Phonics needs.

Use the pre-assessment to identify the skills your students need to master.

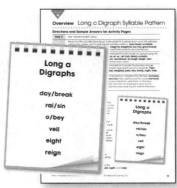

2. MODEL the skill.

Every five-day unit targets a specific phonetic element. On Day 1, use the teacher prompts and reproducible activity page to introduce and model the skill.

Day 1

3. GUIDE PRACTICE and APPLY.

Use the reproducible practice activities for Days 2, 3, and 4 to build students' understanding and skill-proficiency.

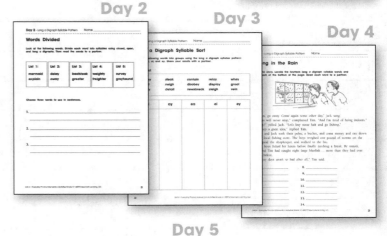

Day 2 **Day 3** **Day 4**

Day 5

4. MONITOR progress.

Administer the Day 5 reproducible assessment to monitor each student's progress and to make instructional decisions.

5. POST-ASSESS to document student progress.

Use the post-assessment to measure students' progress as a result of your interventions.

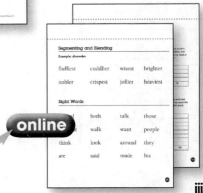

Standards-Based Phonemic Awareness & Phonics Skills in Everyday Intervention Activities

The Phonemic Awareness and Phonics skills found in the Everyday Intervention Activities series are introduced developmentally and spiral from one grade to the next. The chart below shows the skill areas addressed at each grade level in this series.

Everyday Phonics Intervention Activities Series Skills	K	1	2	3	4	5
Phonemic Awareness	✔	✔	✔	✔		
Letter Identification and Formation	✔	✔				
Sound/Symbol Relationships	✔	✔				
Short Vowels		✔				
Consonants		✔				
Long Vowels			✔	✔		
Blends			✔	✔		
Digraphs			✔	✔		
Variant Vowels			✔	✔		
CVCe Syllable Patterns			✔	✔	✔	✔
Closed Syllable Patterns				✔	✔	✔
Open Syllable Patterns				✔	✔	✔
r-Controlled Syllable Patterns				✔	✔	✔
Diphthongs				✔	✔	✔
Silent Letters				✔	✔	✔
Regular and Irregular Plurals				✔	✔	✔
Contractions					✔	✔
Prefixes					✔	✔
Compound Words					✔	✔
Comparatives						✔
Greek and Latin Roots						✔
Homographs and Homophones						✔
Word Origins						✔

Using Everyday Intervention for RTI

According to the National Center on Response to Intervention, RTI "integrates assessment and intervention within a multi-level prevention system to maximize student achievement and to reduce behavior problems." This model of instruction and assessment allows schools to identify at-risk students, monitor their progress, provide research-proven interventions, and "adjust the intensity and nature of those interventions depending on a student's responsiveness."

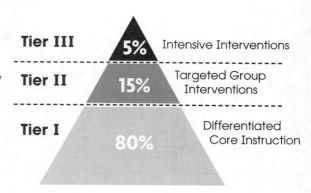

RTI models vary from district to district, but the most prevalent model is a three-tiered approach to instruction and assessment.

The Three Tiers of RTI	Using Everyday Intervention Activities
Tier I: Differentiated Core Instruction • Designed for all students • Preventive, proactive, standards-aligned instruction • Whole- and small-group differentiated instruction • Ninety-minute, daily core reading instruction in the five essential skill areas: phonics, phonemic awareness, comprehension, vocabulary, fluency	• Use whole-group comprehension mini-lessons to introduce and guide practice with comprehension strategies that all students need to learn. • Use any or all of the units in the order that supports your core instructional program.
Tier II: Targeted Group Interventions • For at-risk students • Provide thirty minutes of daily instruction beyond the ninety-minute Tier I core reading instruction • Instruction is conducted in small groups of three to five students with similar needs	• Select units based on your students' areas of need (the pre-assessment can help you identify these). • Use the units as week-long, small-group mini-lessons.
Tier III: Intensive Interventions • For high-risk students experiencing considerable difficulty in reading • Provide up to sixty minutes of additional intensive intervention each day in addition to the ninety-minute Tier I core reading instruction • More intense and explicit instruction • Instruction conducted individually or with smaller groups of one to three students with similar needs	• Select units based on your students' areas of need. • Use the units as one component of an intensive comprehension intervention program.

Overview Closed, VCe, and Open Syllable Patterns

Directions and Sample Answers for Activity Pages

Day 1	See "Model Closed, VCe, and Open Syllable Patterns" below.
Day 2	Read the title and directions aloud. Invite students to divide each word into syllables using the closed, VCe, and open syllable patterns. (**pub/lish, ton/sil, ho/ly, so/lo, i/rate, mis/take, pre/fix, vi/rus**) Have students read each word and choose three words to use in sentences.
Day 3	Read the title and directions aloud. Invite students to sort words into three groups: closed, VCe, and open syllables. (closed: **hel/met, in/sect, pub/lic;** VCe: **cy/clone, shame/ful, tex/tile;** open: **e/go, co/zy, yo/yo**) Have students read each word.
Day 4	Read the title and directions aloud. Invite students to divide the words into syllables using closed, VCe, and open syllable patterns. Then have students locate the words in the word search. (**cul/prit, tab/let, cra/zy, ba/by, rep/tile, re/cite, bo/gus, o/pen**)
Day 5	Read the directions aloud. Allow time for students to complete the first task. (**sub/mit, men/tal, ti/dy, ha/lo, re/late, fruc/tose**). Next, pronounce the words **publish, solo, amaze,** and **mistake** and ask students to write them on the lines. Afterward, meet individually with students. Ask them to read each word on the assessment page. Discuss their results. Use their responses to plan further instruction and review.

Model Closed, VCe, and Open Syllable Patterns

◆ Hand out the Day 1 activity page.

◆ **Say:** *Let's review what we know about closed, VCe, and open syllables.*

◆ Write **pumpkin** on the board and ask students to say the word. Point out that **pumpkin** is a two-syllable word.

◆ **Say:** *I can divide this word into syllables. I will circle the two vowels. We see three consonants between the vowels, but **mp** is a consonant blend and I can't divide consonant blends. I'll divide the word between **p** and **k**: **pump/kin**. Copy what I did on your paper.* Point out that both syllables end with consonants and have a single vowel, so they are both closed syllables.

◆ **Say:** *Now I want to read this word. Since vowel sounds in closed syllables are often short, I'll try the short sounds first.* Model reading the two parts of the word and blending them together: **/pump/ /kin/, pumpkin**.

◆ Repeat with **reptile (rep/tile), silo (si/lo), amaze (a/maze), totem (to/tem)** and **sinus (si/nus)**. Explain that many words have both open and closed syllables.

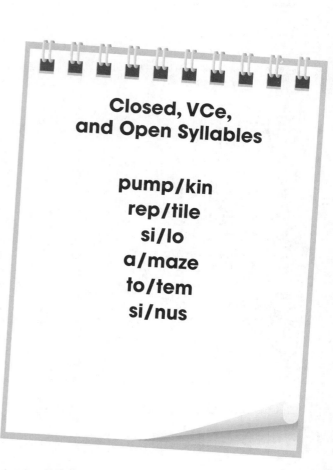

Closed, VCe, and Open Syllables

pump/kin
rep/tile
si/lo
a/maze
to/tem
si/nus

Divide each word into two syllables using closed, VCe, and open syllable patterns.

pumpkin

_____

reptile

_____

silo

_____

amaze

_____

totem

_____

sinus

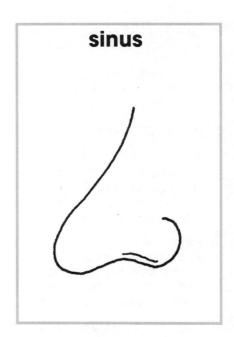

_____

Words Divided

Look at the following words. Divide each word into two syllables using closed, open, VCe, and open/closed syllable patterns. Then read the words to a partner.

List 1: Closed	List 2: Open	List 3: VCe	List 4: Open/Closed
publish	holy	irate	prefix
tonsil	solo	mistake	virus

Choose three words. Use each word in a sentence.

1. _____

_____

2. _____

_____

3. _____

_____

Syllable Sort

Sort the following words into three groups: closed, VCe, and open syllable patterns.
Divide each word into syllables and share your results with a partner.

ego	cozy	cyclone	shameful	yo-yo
textile	helmet	public	insect	

Closed syllables	VCe syllables	Open syllables

Word Search

Divide the words into open and closed syllables. Then locate the words in the word search.

culprit	crazy	reptile	bogus
tablet	baby	recite	open

```
c  r  a  z  y  f  r  e
g  u  r  h  i  d  m  o
e  l  l  b  r  o  t  p
t  r  e  p  t  i  l  e
i  h  y  q  r  s  p  n
c  n  b  l  d  i  g  p
e  t  a  b  l  e  t  r
r  x  b  o  g  u  s  y
```

Assessment

Divide the following words into syllables using closed, VCe, and open syllable patterns.

submit	tidy	relate
mental	halo	fructose

Closed syllables	VCe syllables	Open syllables

Listen to your teacher say each word. Write the word on the line.

1. _____

2. _____

3. _____

4. _____

Overview Long a and o Digraphs Syllable Patterns

Directions and Sample Answers for Activity Pages

Day 1	See "Model Long a and o Digraphs Syllable Patterns" below.
Day 2	Read the title and directions aloud. Invite students to divide each word into syllables using the closed, open, and long **a** and **o** digraph syllable patterns. (**ob/tain, birth/day, jail/break, eight/een, sur/vey, a/float, woe/ful, dis/own**) Have students read each word and choose three words to use in sentences.
Day 3	Read the title and directions aloud. Invite students to sort words into two groups: long **a** and long **o**. (long **a**: **qu<u>ai</u>nt, spr<u>ai</u>n, fr<u>ay</u>, pr<u>ey</u>, gr<u>ea</u>t, br<u>ea</u>k, n<u>eigh</u>, sl<u>eigh</u>, wh<u>ey</u>, gr<u>ay</u>**; long **o**: **r<u>oa</u>m, m<u>oa</u>n, mistlet<u>oe</u>, f<u>oe</u>, s<u>ow</u>n, st<u>ow</u>**) Have students underline the long **a** and **o** digraphs and then read each word.
Day 4	Read the title and directions aloud. Invite students to read each word and each sentence. Have students fill in the blanks with the correct word. (**windblown, Steakhouse, overpaid, whey, stagecoach, eight, tippy-toe, stingray**)
Day 5	Read the directions aloud. Allow time for students to complete the first task. (**re/tail, high/way, out/break, sur/vey, char/coal, a/glow**). Next, pronounce the words **eighty, daybreak, foe** and **rainbow**. Ask students to write them on the lines. Afterward, meet individually with students. Ask them to read each word on the assessment page. Discuss their results. Use their responses to plan further instruction and review.

Model Long a and o Digraphs Syllable Patterns

◆ Hand out the Day 1 activity page.

◆ **Say:** *Let's look at different ways to write long **a** and long **o** sounds.*

◆ Write **explain** on the board and ask students to say the word. **Say:** *Ai is another way to make the long **a** sound.* Point out that **explain** is a two-syllable word.

◆ **Say:** *Watch as I divide this word into syllables. I will circle the three vowels. We see three consonants between the vowels, but **pl** is a consonant blend and I can't divide consonant blends. I'll divide the word between the **x** and **p**: **ex/plain**. Copy what I did on your paper.* Point out that both syllables end with consonants so they are closed syllables.

◆ **Say:** *Now I want to read this word. Look at the first syllable. Since vowel sounds in closed syllables are often short, I'll try the short sound first. The second syllable has **ai** in it, and I know **ai** makes the long **a** sound.* Model reading the two parts of the word and blending them together: **/ex/ /plān/, explain.**

◆ Repeat with other long a digraphs: **ay, ea, eigh, ey** in the words **daybreak, weightless,** and **obey.**

◆ Then repeat with long o digraphs **oa, oe,** and **ow** found in the words: **cockroach, toenail,** and **rainbow.**

Long *a* and Long *o* Syllables

ex/pl<u>ai</u>n
day/br<u>ea</u>k
w<u>eigh</u>t/less
o/b<u>ey</u>
cock/r<u>oa</u>ch
t<u>oe</u>/nail
r<u>ai</u>n/b<u>ow</u>

Divide the following words into syllables. Underline the long *a* or long *o* sound in each word.

explain

daybreak

weightless

obey

_____　_____　_____　_____

cockroach

toenail

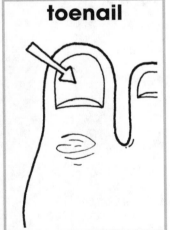

rainbow

_____　_____　_____

Words Divided

Look at the following words. Divide each word into two syllables using closed, open, and long *a* and *o* syllable patterns. Then read the words to a partner.

List 1:

obtain _____

birthday _____

jailbreak _____

eighteen _____

survey _____

List 2:

afloat _____

woeful _____

disown _____

Choose three words. Use each word in a sentence.

1. _____

_____

2. _____

_____

3. _____

_____

Syllable Sort

Sort the following words into two groups: long *a* and long *o* syllable patterns. Underline the long *a* and *o* digraphs and then read each word to a partner.

quaint	stow	sown	great
roam	gray	fray	sleigh
break	sprain	moan	mistletoe
prey	neigh	foe	whey

Long a digraphs	**Long o digraphs**

Unit 2 • Everyday Phonics Intervention Activities Grade 5 • © Newmark Learning, LLC

Fill In the Blank

Read the words in the box. Then read the sentences. Fill in the blanks with the appropriate word.

overpaid	Steakhouse	whey	tippy-toe
stingray	eight	stagecoach	windblown

My hair is _____.

Tony's _____ is the best place to eat.

Mrs. Jones _____ me for mowing her lawn.

Little Miss Muffet ate curds and _____.

A _____ ride was not very comfortable.

The recipe called for _____ cups of flour

_____ down the hallway so you don't wake your dad.

We saw a _____ in the waters off the Florida coast.

Assessment

Divide the following words into syllables using open, closed, long _a_, and long _o_ syllable patterns.

retail   _____

highway   _____

outbreak   _____

survey   _____

charcoal   _____

aglow   _____

Listen to your teacher say each word. Write the word on the line.

1. _____   3. _____

2. _____   4. _____

Overview Long e and i Digraphs Syllable Patterns

Directions and Sample Answers for Activity Pages

Day 1	See "Model Long e and i Digraphs Syllable Patterns" below.
Day 2	Read the title and directions aloud. Invite students to divide each word into syllables using the closed, open, and long **e** and **i** digraph syllable patterns. (**re/veal, oat/meal, don/key, wind/shield, neck/tie, de/nied, re/plies, mid/night**) Have students read each word and choose three words to use in sentences.
Day 3	Read the title and directions aloud. Invite students to sort words into two groups: long **e** digraphs and long **i** digraphs. (long **e**: **conceal, release, esteem, parakeet, key, galley, belief, thief**; long **i**: **terrified, necktie, thigh, higher**) Have students underline the long **e** and **i** digraphs and then read each word.
Day 4	Read the title and directions aloud. Invite students to unscramble the sentences and write them on the lines. Then have students draw a picture that shows what is happening in each sentence. Have students read each sentence to a partner. (A magician can disappear and reappear. I hurt my back while doing a cartwheel. Volleyball is my favorite sport. A timepiece is like a watch. My $20 coupon was applied to the total. My eyesight is not very good at night.)
Day 5	Read the directions aloud. Allow time for students to complete the first task. (**moon/beam, pre/teen, gal/ley, a/piece, re/lied, in/sight**). Next, pronounce the words **conceal, esteem, donkey, thief, necktie,** and **higher** and ask students to write them on the lines. Afterward, meet individually with students. Ask them to read each word on the assessment page. Discuss their results. Use their responses to plan further instruction and review.

Model Long e and i Digraphs Syllable Patterns

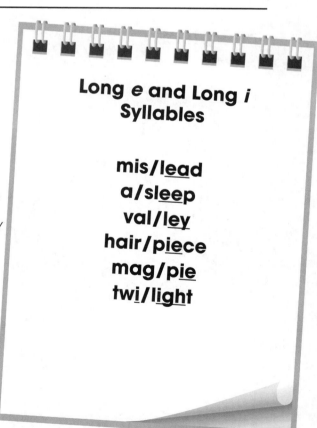

Long e and Long i Syllables

mis/le<u>a</u>d
a/sl<u>ee</u>p
val/l<u>ey</u>
hair/p<u>ie</u>ce
mag/p<u>ie</u>
tw<u>i</u>/l<u>igh</u>t

◆ Hand out the Day 1 activity page.

◆ **Say:** *Let's look at different ways to write the long e and long i sounds.*

◆ Write **mislead** on the board and ask students to say the word. **Say:** *Ea is another way to make the long e sound.* Point out that **mislead** is a two-syllable word.

◆ **Say:** *Watch as I divide this word into syllables. I will circle the three vowels. We see two consonants between the vowels, so I'll divide the word between the s and l: mis/lead. Copy what I did on your paper.* Point out that both syllables end with consonants, so they are both closed syllables.

◆ **Say:** *Now I want to read this word. The first syllable is a closed syllable. Closed syllables usually make the short vowel sound, so I'll try the short i sound first. The second syllable has ea in it, and I know ea makes the long e sound.* Model reading the two parts of the word and blending them together: **/mis/ /lēd/, mislead.**

◆ Repeat with long **e** digraphs **ee, ey,** and **ie** in **asleep, valley, hairpiece.**

◆ Then repeat with long **i** digraphs **ie** and **igh** in **magpie** and **twilight (mag/pie, twi/light).**

Divide the following words into syllables. Underline the long *e* or long *i* sound in each word.

mislead

_____

asleep

_____

valley

_____

hairpiece

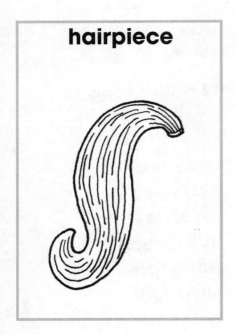

_____

magpie

_____

twilight

_____

Words Divided

Look at the following words. Divide each word into two syllables using closed, open, and long *e* and *i* syllable patterns. Then read the words to a partner.

List 1:

reveal   _____

oatmeal   _____

donkey   _____

windshield   _____

List 2:

necktie   _____

denied   _____

replies   _____

midnight   _____

Choose three words. Use each word in a sentence.

1. _____

_____

2. _____

_____

3. _____

_____

Syllable Sort

Sort the following words into two groups: long *e* and long *i* digraphs. Underline the long *e* and long *i* digraphs and then read each word to a partner.

terrified	thief	esteem	release
parakeet	necktie	belief	higher
conceal	key	thigh	galley

Long e digraphs | **Long i digraphs**

Sentence Scramble

Unscramble the sentences and write them on the lines. Then draw a picture that shows what is happening in each sentence. Read your sentences to a partner.

can A disappear and magician reappear.

_____

_____

_____

cartwheel I doing a back while hurt my

_____

_____

_____

favorite is sport my Volleyball

_____

_____

_____

like timepiece A watch is a

_____

_____

_____

total was My coupon $20 to applied the

_____

_____

_____

night is good My very at eyesight not

_____

_____

_____

Assessment

Divide the following words into syllables using open, closed, long *e*, and long *i* syllable patterns.

moonbeam _____

preteen _____

galley _____

apiece _____

relied _____

insight _____

Listen to your teacher say each word. Write the word on the line.

1. _____　　　4. _____

2. _____　　　5. _____

3. _____　　　6. _____

Overview r-Controlled a and o Syllable Patterns

Directions and Sample Answers for Activity Pages

Day 1	See "Model r-Controlled a and o Syllable Patterns" below.
Day 2	Read the title and directions aloud. Invite students to divide each word into syllables using the closed, open, and **r**-controlled a, /âr/, and o syllable patterns. (**mar/ket, jar/gon, de/spair, wear/ing, com/pare, flor/al, soar/ing, four/teen, floor/ing**) Have students read each word and choose three words to use in sentences.
Day 3	Read the title and directions aloud. Invite students to sort words into three groups: **r**-controlled **/är/** as in **car**, **r**-controlled **/âr/** as in **air**, and **r**-controlled **/ô/** as in **more**. (**r**-controlled **/är/: regards, pardon; r**-controlled **/âr/: repair, prairie, pear, tear, warfare, flare; r**-controlled **/ô/: sordid, consort, hoarding, boar, mourning, resource**)
Day 4	Read the title and directions aloud. Invite students to complete the crossword puzzle using the clues and words in the box. (Across: 1. **wear**, 3. **square**, 4. **garden**, 8. **soar**, 9. **stars**. Down: 2. **repair**, 5. **door**, 6. **normal**, 7. **court**.)
Day 5	Read the directions aloud. Allow time for students to complete the first task. (**tar/get, fair/ly, swear/ing, pre/pare, pear, fort/ress, hoard/er, trap/door, court/ship**) Next, pronounce the words **hairy, wear, compare, formal, soaring,** and **indoors** and ask students to write them on the lines. Afterward, meet individually with students. Ask them to read each word on the assessment page. Discuss their results. Use their responses to plan further instruction and review.

Model r-Controlled a and o Syllable Patterns

◆ Hand out the Day 1 activity page.

◆ Write **starry** on the board and ask students to say the word. Circle the **ar**. Say: *The letters **ar** in the middle of **starry** sound like /är/ as in car. The vowel sound is neither long nor short. When the letter **r** follows a vowel, it affects, or controls, the sound that the vowel stands for. These syllables are called **r**-controlled.*

◆ **Say:** *When words with **r**-controlled vowels are divided into syllables, the vowel plus the **r** usually stay in the same syllable. I also know that words with double consonants are divided between the consonants. I'll divide the word between the double letters: **star/ry**. Copy what I did on your paper.*

◆ **Say:** *Now I want to read this word. The first syllable is closed, but it is also **r**-controlled. I think this syllable should sound like /är/ as in car. The second syllable is open. I know open syllables often make the long vowel sound, and **y** is one way to make the long **e** sound. I'll try the long vowel sound first.* Model reading the two parts of the word and blending them together: /stär/ /rē/, starry.

◆ Repeat with **r**-controlled **/âr/** syllable patterns: **-air, -ear, -are** in **fairy, teddy bear, beware,** and **pear**. Then repeat with **r**-controlled **/ô/** syllable patterns: **or, oar, oor,** and **our: record, aboard, indoors,** and **pouring.**

r-Controlled /är/, /âr/, and /ô/

star/ry

f<u>air</u>/y

ted/dy b<u>ear</u>

be/w<u>are</u>

p<u>ear</u>

re/c<u>or</u>d

a/b<u>oar</u>d

in/d<u>oor</u>s

p<u>our</u>/ing

Divide the following words into syllables. Underline the _r_-controlled sound in each word.

starry

_____

fairy

_____

teddy bear

_____

beware

_____

pear

_____

record

_____

All aboard!

_____

indoors

_____

pouring

_____

Words Divided

Look at the following words. Divide each word into two syllables using closed, open, and r-controlled *a*, /âr/, and *o* syllable patterns. Then read the words to a partner.

List 1:

market   _____

jargon   _____

List 3:

floral   _____

soaring   _____

List 2:

despair   _____

wearing   _____

fourteen   _____

flooring   _____

compare   _____

Choose three words. Use each word in a sentence.

1. _____

_____

2. _____

_____

3. _____

_____

Syllable Sort

Sort the following words into three groups: r-controlled _är_ as in _car_, /âr/ as in _air_, and ô as in _more_. Read each word to a partner.

resource	warfare	flare	consort	prairie
tear	sordid	hoarding	pear	boar
repair	regards	pardon	mourning	

r-controlled **är** as in _car_	r-controlled **/âr/** as in _air_	r-controlled **ô** as in _more_

Crossword Puzzle

Complete the crossword puzzle using the clues and the words in the box.

stars	normal
garden	soar
repair	door
court	wear
square	

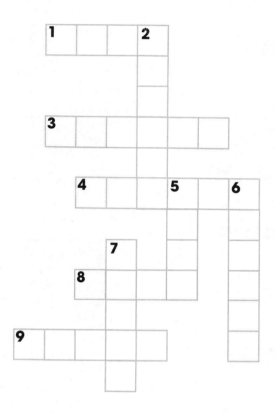

Clues

Across

1. You _____ clothes to school.

3. A four-sided object with equal sides

4. Carrots grow in our _____.

8. Eagles _____ in the sky.

9. At night, the sky is filled
   with _____.

Down

2. to fix something

5. Open the _____.

6. Not abnormal, but _____

7. A king and queen live at their _____.

Name _____

Assessment

Divide the following words into syllables using closed, closed, r-controlled *är*, */âr/*, and *ô* syllable patterns.

target _____

fairly _____

swearing _____

prepare _____

pear _____

fortress _____

hoarder _____

trapdoor _____

courtship _____

Listen to your teacher say each word. Write the word on the line.

1. _____   4. _____

2. _____   5. _____

3. _____   6. _____

Overview r-Controlled e, i, and u Syllable Patterns

Directions and Sample Answers for Activity Pages

Day 1	See "Model r-Controlled e, i, and u Syllable Patterns" below.
Day 2	Read the title and directions aloud. Invite students to divide each word into syllables using the closed, open, and r-controlled **e**, **i**, and **u** syllable patterns. (**as/sert, cer/tain, con/cert, birth/day, skirm/ish, thirst/y, bur/den, bur/lap, cur/tain**) Have students read each word and choose three words to use in sentences.
Day 3	Read the title and directions aloud. Invite students to sort words into three groups: r-controlled **e** as in **fern**, r-controlled **i** as in **bird**, and r-controlled **u** as in **hurt**. (**r-controlled e: winter, vertical, sterling; r-controlled i: whirlwind, dirty, twirling; r-controlled u: urgent, urban, turnip**)
Day 4	Read the title and directions aloud. Invite students to cut out the sentence parts and then put the parts together to form sentences that make sense. Have students glue correctly formed sentences onto a piece of notebook paper. (A verb is an action word. Ouch! That medicine burns my arm. The waitress served our food. My uncle joined the Merchant Marines. My aunt turned thirty on her last birthday. A smirk is a sneaky smile. The class gave our teacher a surprise party. Please don't squirt water in my face. The nurse brought my medicine to my room.)
Day 5	Read the directions aloud. Allow time for students to complete the first task. (**toast/er, con/cern, a/stir, black/bird, pur/chase, fur/lough**) Next, pronounce the words **concert, thirsty,** and **burden** and ask students to write them on the lines. Afterward, meet individually with students. Ask them to read each word on the assessment page. Discuss their results. Use their responses to plan further instruction and review.

Model r-Controlled e, i, and u Syllable Patterns

◆ Hand out the Day 1 activity page.

◆ Write **purr** on the board. Ask students to say the word. Point out that **purr** has one closed syllable. Have students circle **ur**. **Say:** *The letters **ur** in the middle of **purr** sound like **fur**. The vowel sound is neither long nor short. When the letter **r** follows a vowel, it affects, or controls, the sound that the vowel stands for. These syllables are called **r**-controlled. You can use what you know about letter patterns and syllables to read longer words.*

◆ Write **perfect** on the board. **Say:** *I will circle the **e** vowels. When words with **r**-controlled vowels are divided into syllables, the vowel plus the **r** usually stay in the same syllable. I'll divide the word between the **r** and **f**: **per/fect**. Copy what I did on your paper.*

◆ **Say:** *Now I want to read this word. The first syllable is closed, but it is also **r**-controlled. I think this syllable should sound like /ûr/ as in **purr**. The second syllable is also closed. I know closed syllables make the short vowel sound, so I'll try that sound first. Model reading the two parts of the word and blending them together: /pûr/ /fect/, perfect.*

◆ Repeat with **awhirl** and **unfurl**. Point out that **ir** and **ur** can make the /ûr/ sound as in **purr**.

**r-Controlled
e, i, and u Syllables**

p**er**/fect

a/wh**ir**l

un/f**ur**l

Divide the following words into syllables. Underline the *r*-controlled sound in each word.

perfect	awhirl	unfurl

_____   _____   _____

Words Divided

Look at the following words. Divide each word into two syllables using closed, open, and *r*-controlled *e, i,* and *u* syllable patterns. Then read the words to a partner.

List 1:	List 2:	List 3:
assert	birthday	burden
certain	skirmish	burlap
concert	thirsty	curtain

Choose three words. Use each word in a sentence.

1. _____

_____

2. _____

_____

3. _____

_____

Syllable Sort

Sort the following words into three groups: *r-controlled e* as in *fern*, *i* as in *bird*, and *u* as in *hurt*. Read each word to a partner.

turnip	dirty	urban	urgent	vertical
winter	sterling	whirlwind	twirling	

r-controlled e as in *fern*	r-controlled i as in *bird*	r-controlled u as in *hurt*

Sentence Scramble

Cut out the sentence parts and then put the parts together to form sentences that make sense. Glue correctly formed sentences onto a piece of notebook paper. Read the sentences to a partner.

A verb is	a sneaky smile.
Ouch! That medicine	a surprise party.
The waitress	water in my face.
My uncle joined	burns my arm.
My aunt turned thirty	my medicine to my room.
A smirk is	on her last birthday.
The class gave our teacher	served our food.
Please don't squirt	the Merchant Marines.
The nurse brought	an action word.

Assessment

Divide the following words into syllables using closed, open, *r*-controlled *e*, *i*, and *u* syllable patterns.

toaster _____

concern _____

astir _____

blackbird _____

purchase _____

furlough _____

Listen to your teacher say each word. Write the word on the line.

1. _____

2. _____

3. _____

Overview Vowel Diphthong /oi/ and /ou/ Syllable Patterns

Directions and Sample Answers for Activity Pages

Day 1	See "Model Vowel Diphthong /oi/ and /ou/ Syllable Patterns" below.
Day 2	Read the title and directions aloud. Invite students to divide each word into syllables using the closed, open, and vowel diphthong /oi/ and /ou/ syllable patterns. (tur/moil, re/coil, en/joy, a/hoy, dis/count, pro/nounce, down/town, eye/brow) Have students read each word and choose three words to use in sentences.
Day 3	Read the title and directions aloud. Invite students to sort words into two groups: vowel diphthong /oi/ and /ou/. (/oi/: hard-boil, joint, viewpoint, overjoy, coy, destroy; /ou/: pounce, account, dormouse, prowl, fowl, meltdown)
Day 4	Read the title and directions aloud. Invite students to use a dictionary to define the vowel diphthong /oi/ and /ou/ syllable words. Match them to the correct description and then locate the words in the word search. (soy, coil, prowl, ploy, surround, turquoise, paramount, renown)
Day 5	Read the directions aloud. Allow time for students to complete the first task. (moist/en, an/noy, a/stound, prowl/er) Next, pronounce the words noisy, enjoy, grouchy, and shower and ask students to write them on the lines. Afterward, meet individually with students. Ask them to read each word on the assessment page. Discuss their results. Use their responses to plan further instruction and review.

Model Vowel Diphthong /oi/ and /ou/ Syllable Patterns

◆ Hand out the Day 1 activity page.

◆ Write **coin** on the board and ask students to say the word. Point out that **coin** has one closed syllable. Have students circle **oi**. **Say:** *The letters oi in the middle of* **coin** *sound like* **join**. *Notice that the vowel sound is neither long nor short. You can use what you know about letter patterns and syllables to read longer words.*

◆ Write **noisy** on the board. **Say:** *I will circle the vowels* **oi** *and* **y**. *Since* **nois** *is part of the base word* **noise**, *I'll divide the word between the* **s** *and* **y**: **nois/y**. *Copy what I did on your paper.*

◆ **Say:** *Now I want to read this word. The first syllable is closed and has an* /oi/ *in it. That syllable probably sounds like* **coin**. *I'll try that vowel sound first. The second syllable is open and ends in a* **y**. *Y syllables usually make the long* **e** *sound, so I'll try that vowel sound first.* Model reading the two parts of the word and blending them together: /nois//ē/, noisy.

◆ Repeat with the /oi/ sound in **employ**.

◆ Then repeat with /ou/ sounds (as in **house**) in the words **grouchy** and **shower**.

Vowel Diphthong /oi/ and /ou/ Syllables

nois/y
em/ploy
grouch/y
show/er

e the following words into syllables. Underline the */oi/* sound, as in *coin*.

noisy

_____

employ

_____

Divide the following words into syllables. Underline the */ou/* sound, as in *house*.

grouchy

_____

shower

_____

Words Divided

Look at the following words. Divide each word into two syllables using closed, open, and vowel diphthong /oi/ and /ou/ syllable patterns. Then read the words to a partner.

List 1: /oi/ words

turmoil _____

recoil _____

enjoy _____

ahoy _____

List 2: /ou/ words

discount _____

pronounce _____

downtown _____

eyebrow _____

Choose three words. Use each word in a sentence.

1. _____

_____

2. _____

_____

3. _____

_____

Syllable Sort

Sort the following words into two groups: vowel diphthong */oi/* and */ou/*.
Read each word to a partner.

prowl	joint	coy	fowl
hard-boil	overjoy	meltdown	account
dormouse	pounce	viewpoint	destroy

/oi/ as in *coin* and *boy*	/ou/ as in *bounce* and *howl*

Word Search

Use a dictionary to define these vowel diphthong *oi* and *ou* words; then match the words to their descriptions. Then find the words in the word search.

prowl	coil	surround	soy
paramount	ploy	turquoise	renown

1. a type of bean: _____

2. to make a tight ring: _____

3. to sneak around looking for something: _____

4. a plan or plot: _____

5. to extend all the way around: _____

6. a type of mineral often used in jewelry: _____

7. very important: _____

8. fame: _____

```
p  e  s  i  o  u  q  r  u  t
q  l  t  r  r  e  n  o  w  n
l  d  o  u  m  s  v  j  y  a
w  w  o  y  x  l  l  i  o  c
o  d  n  u  o  r  r  u  s  w
r  r  p  l  h  o  b  d  v  m
p  a  r  a  m  o  u  n  t  z
```

Assessment

Divide the following words into syllables using open, closed, and vowel diphthong /oi/ and /ou/ syllable patterns.

moisten _____

annoy _____

astound _____

prowler _____

Listen to your teacher say each word. Write the word on the line.

1. _____   3. _____

2. _____   4. _____

Overview Vowel Diphthong /o͞o/, /o͝o/, and /ô/ Syllable Patterns

Directions and Sample Answers for Activity Pages

Day 1	See "Model Vowel Diphthong /o͞o/, /o͝o/, and /ô/ Syllable Patterns" below.
Day 2	Read the title and directions aloud. Invite students to divide each word into syllables using the closed, open, and vowel diphthong /o͞o/, /o͝o/, and /ô/ syllable patterns. (**sa/loon, soup/y, cur/few, pur/sue, red/wood, rose/bush, odd/ball, haunt/ed, with/drawn, froth/y**) Have students read each word and choose three words to use in sentences.
Day 3	Read the title and directions aloud. Invite students to sort words into three groups: vowel diphthong /o͞o/, /o͝o/, and /ô/ syllable patterns. (**/o͞o/: spoof, croup, renew, hue**; **/o͝o/: rook, nook, bull, rosebush**; **/ô/: squall, fraught, outlaw, froth**)
Day 4	Read the title and directions aloud. Invite students to read each word and each sentence. Have students fill in the blanks with the correct word. (**interview, afoot, naughty, moss, swooped, residue, croupy, pinball, push, caw**)
Day 5	Read the directions aloud. Allow time for students to complete the first task. (**la/goon, out/grew, re/vue, un/hook, ap/pall, as/sault, ob/long**) Next, pronounce the words **cartoon, regroup, ambush, install**, and **defrost** and ask students to write them on the lines. Afterward, meet individually with students. Ask them to read each word on the assessment page. Discuss their results. Use their responses to plan further instruction and review.

Model Vowel Diphthong /o͞o/, /o͝o/, and /ô/ Syllable Patterns

Vowel Diphthong /o͞o/, /o͝o/, and /ô/ Syllable Patterns

rac/coon
re/group
cash/ew
pur/sue
book/mark
am/bush
in/stall
dis/traught
jig/saw
de/frost

◆ Hand out the Day 1 activity page.

◆ Write **raccoon** on the board and ask students to say the word. Point out that **raccoon** has two syllables. Have students circle **o͞o**. **Say:** *The letters **oo** in the second syllable sound like **soon**. The vowel sound is neither long nor short.*

◆ **Say:** *I will circle the vowels **a** and **oo**. There are double consonants between the vowels, so I'll divide the word between them: **rac/coon**. Copy what I did on your paper.*

◆ **Say:** *Now I want to read this word. The first syllable is closed, so it probably has a short vowel sound. The second syllable is also closed but has an **oo** in it. This syllable should make the sound like **soon**.* Model reading the two parts of the word and blending them together: **/rac/ /co͞on/**.

◆ Repeat with **regroup, cashew**, and **pursue**. Point out that **ou, ew**, and **ue** can make the same sound as in **soon**. Identify syllables as open or closed.

◆ Next repeat with **o͝o** words as in **took**. (**bookmark, ambush**)

◆ Then repeat with **ô** words as **all**. (**install, distraught, jigsaw**, and **defrost**) Point out that **au, aw**, and **o** can make the same sound as **a** in **call**. Identify syllables as open or closed.

Divide the following words into syllables. Underline the /o͞o/ sound in each word, as in *soon*.

raccoon	regroup	cashew	pursue
		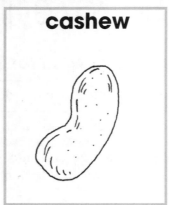	

_____ _____ _____ _____

Divide the following words into syllables. Underline the /o͝o/ sound in each word, as in *push*.

bookmark	ambush

_____ _____

Divide the following words into syllables. Underline the /ô/ sound in each word, as in *tall*.

install	distraught	jigsaw	defrost
		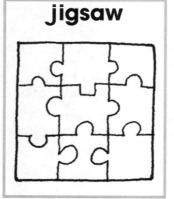	

_____ _____ _____ _____

Words Divided

Look at the following words. Divide each word into two syllables using closed, open, and vowel diphthong /o͞o/, /o͝o/, and /ô/ syllable patterns. Then read the words to a partner.

List 1: /o͞o/ words	**List 2: /o͝o/ words**	**List 3: /ô/ words**
saloon	redwood	oddball
soupy	rosebush	haunted
curfew		withdrawn
pursue		frothy

Choose three words. Use each word in a sentence.

1. _____

_____

2. _____

_____

3. _____

_____

Syllable Sort

Sort the following words into three groups: vowel diphthong /o͞o/, /o͝o/, and /ô/. Read each word to a partner.

spoof	froth	fraught	croup
bull	nook	hue	outlaw
squall	renew	rook	rosebush

/o͞o/ as in *soon* and *brew*	/o͝o/ as in *cook* and *full*	/ô/ as in *crawl* and *lost*

Fill in the Blank

Read the words in the box. Then read the sentences. Fill in the blanks with the appropriate word.

swooped	push
croupy	pinball
interview	naughty
residue	caw
afoot	moss

The president's _____ was replayed on TV.

The game is _____.

My little brother was very _____ when he broke my toy.

_____ grows in wet climates.

The eagle _____ down and caught the mouse in her talons.

Cheap glass cleaner sometimes leaves a _____ on mirrors.

A _____ cough sounds like a barking seal.

I love to play _____ games.

_____ the wheelbarrow up the ramp.

Blackbirds say _____.

Assessment

Divide the following words into syllables using closed, open, and vowel diphthong /o͞o/, /o͝o/, and /ô/ syllable patterns.

lagoon _____

outgrew _____

revue _____

unhook _____

appall _____

assault _____

oblong _____

Listen to your teacher say each word. Write the word on the line.

1. _____   4. _____

2. _____   5. _____

3. _____

Overview Consonant + le, al, el Words

Directions and Sample Answers for Activity Pages

Day 1	See "Model Consonant + le, al, el Words" below.
Day 2	Read the title and directions aloud. Invite students to divide each word into syllables using open and closed syllable patterns. (**cod/dle, knuck/le, gris/tle, feu/dal, glob/al, rent/al, chis/el, swiv/el, yo/kel**) Have students read each word and choose three words to use in sentences.
Day 3	Read the title and directions aloud. Invite students to sort words into the three word groups: consonant **+ le**, consonant **+ al**, and consonant **+ el**. (**le: angle, tussle, sickle; al: mental, jackal, legal; el: chapel, rebel, drivel**) Have students choose three unknown words and define them using a dictionary.
Day 4	Read the title and directions aloud. Invite students to use the consonant **+ le, al**, and **el** endings to finish the words. (**focal, snivel, duffle, heckle, dental, nickel**) Then have students choose three words and write them in sentences.
Day 5	Read the directions aloud. Allow time for students to complete the first task. (**tur/tle, cym/bal, stru/del, sig/nal, fid/dle, re/pel**). Next, pronounce the words **angle, global**, and **rebel** and ask students to write them on the lines. Afterward, meet individually with students. Ask them to read each word on the assessment page. Discuss their results. Use their responses to plan further instruction and review.

Model Consonant + le, al, and el Words

◆ Hand out the Day 1 activity page.

◆ Write **maple, regal, kernel** on the board. Have students circle the **le, al**, and **el**. **Say:** *Words that end in -le, -al, and -el all stand for the same sound. /+ l/ (pronounced /ul/). These letter pairs and the consonant that comes before them usually form the last syllable in a word.*

◆ **Say:** *Look at* **maple**. *I know that* **ple** *forms the last syllable. So the first syllable must be* **ma**. *(ma/ple) Copy what I did on your paper.*

◆ **Say:** *Now I want to read* **maple**. *The first syllable is open so it should have a long* **a** *sound. I'll try that first. The second syllable makes the /pl/ sound. Model reading the two parts of the word and blending them together: /ma/ /pl/.*

◆ Repeat with **regal** and **kernel**. (**re/gal, ker/nel**) Identify syllables as opened or closed. Model reading the two words: **/rē/ /gal/, /kûr/ /nel/.**

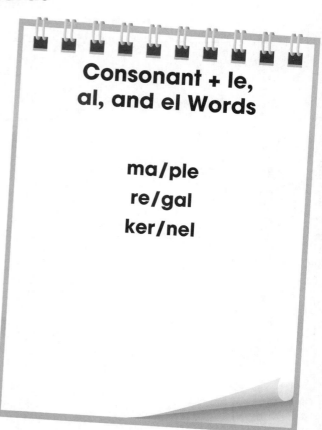

Consonant + le, al, and el Words

ma/ple
re/gal
ker/nel

Divide the following words into syllables.

maple	regal	kernel
		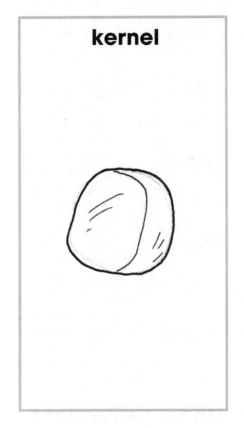

_____   _____   _____

Name _____

Words Divided

Look at the following words. Use a dictionary to divide each consonant + *le*, *al*, and *el* word into syllables. Then read the words to a partner.

List 1:	List 2:	List 3:
coddle	feudal	chisel
knuckle	global	swivel
gristle	rental	yokel

Choose three words. Use each word in a sentence.

1. _____

_____

2. _____

_____

3. _____

_____

Consonant + le, al, el Word Sort

Sort the following words into groups using consonant + *le*, *al*, and *el*. Share your results with a partner.

mental	chapel	sickle	tussle	drivel
angle	legal	rebel	jackal	

le	al	el

Use a dictionary to define three words that you do not know. Write the definitions on the lines below.

1. _____

_____

2. _____

_____

3. _____

_____

Add the Ending

Use the consonant + *le*, *al*, and *el* endings to finish the words.

fle	**tal**	**vel**
ckle	**cal**	**ckel**

fo___   he___

sni___   den___

duf___   ni___

Choose three words and write them in sentences.

1. _____

_____

2. _____

_____

3. _____

_____

Assessment

Divide the following words into syllables.

turtle _____

cymbal _____

strudel _____

signal _____

fiddle _____

repel _____

Listen to your teacher say each word. Write the word on the line.

1. _____

2. _____

3. _____

Overview Compound Words

Directions and Sample Answers for Activity Pages

Day 1	See "Model Compound Words" below.
Day 2	Read the title and directions aloud. Invite students to sort words into the three compound word groups: open, closed, and hyphenated. (**open: air bag, living room, poison ivy, sea gull; closed: flowerpot, wheelchair, mousetrap, rooftop; hyphenated: know-how, house-to-house, passer-by, merry-go-round**) Have students read each word.
Day 3	Read the title and directions aloud. Invite students to draw literal interpretations of each compound word. Have students read each word and use them in sentences.
Day 4	Read the title and directions aloud. Invite students to answer the riddles and closed sentences using words from the compound word list. (**A southpaw, There wasn't mushroom, A hot dog, They are two-tired, pork chops, tightrope, high-rise, step-by-step**)
Day 5	Read the directions aloud. Allow time for students to complete the first task. (**step-by-step, pork chops, bedroll, merry-go-round, sea gull, dugout**). Next, pronounce the words **fire drill, scarecrow,** and **house-to-house** and ask students to write them on the lines. Afterward, meet individually with students. Ask them to read each word on the assessment page. Discuss their results. Use their responses to plan further instruction and review.

Model Compound Words

◆ Hand out the Day 1 activity page.

◆ Write **fire drill, dugout,** and **sing-along** on the board and read them aloud.

◆ **Say:** *These words are all compound words. There are three types of compound words. Open compound words like **fire drill** are made up of two separate words. Closed compound words like **dugout** are made up of combined words. Hyphenated compound words like **sing-along** are made up of two or more words separated by a hyphen or hyphens.*

◆ Tell students that identifying compound words is easy. When a compound word is divided, each small word must mean something on its own. For example, **dugout** is made up of two small words: **dug** and **out**. Each small word means something.

◆ Help students identify the small words that make up **fire drill** and **sing-along**.

◆ Explain that identifying the meaning of compound words is not as simple as knowing the meanings of the smaller words. The word **doghouse** means a house for a dog. The word **wishbone**, however, is not that simple. If you didn't know the meaning of **wishbone**, you would need a dictionary.

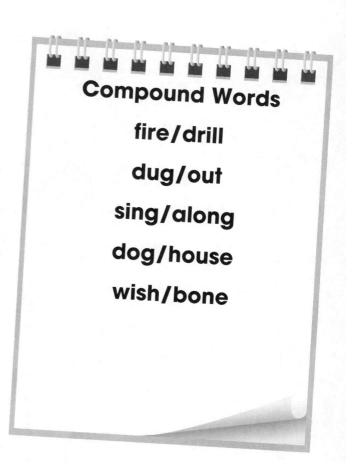

Compound Words

fire/drill

dug/out

sing/along

dog/house

wish/bone

Divide the following compound words into smaller words.

fire drill

dugout

sing-along

_____

is made up of the

words _____

and _____.

_____

is made up of the

words _____

and _____.

_____

is made up of the

words _____

and _____.

doghouse

wishbone

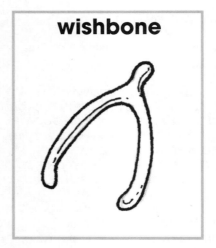

_____

is made up of the

words _____

and _____.

_____

is made up of the

words _____

and _____.

Compound Word Sort

Read the following words. Sort them by the three compound word types: open, closed, and hyphenated. Share your results with a partner.

know-how	**sea gull**	**passer-by**
wheelchair	**house-to-house**	**merry-go-round**
living room	**poison ivy**	**flowerpot**
rooftop	**mousetrap**	**air bag**

Open compound words	Closed compound words	Hyphenated compound words

Can a Bed Roll?

Many compound words do not mean what their smaller words mean. Read the compound words below. Draw the literal meaning of each word. Ask yourself: What does a rolling bed look like? Can a door be a bell? What might a double-cross look like?

bedroll

doorbell

double-cross

Identify the meaning of each word by using a dictionary. Use each word in a sentence.

1. _____

_____

2. _____

_____

3. _____

_____

Using Your Brain

Read the riddles below. Use words from the riddle list to answer the riddles.

What do you call a dog that is left-handed?_____

Why did the fungi leave the room?_____

What kind of dog likes living where it's sunny and warm?_____

Why do bicycles fall over? _____

Riddle List:
There wasn't mushroom.
They are two-tired.
A southpaw
A hot dog

Read the sentences below. Use words from the compound word list to fill in the blanks.

My pig learned karate. Now he's learning _____.

The _____ walker is my favorite part of a circus.

I work in a _____ building.

I can read _____ instructions to tell me how to put this thing together.

Compound Word List:
tightrope
step-by-step
high-rise
pork chops

Assessment

The following compound words are written incorrectly. Write them correctly in the space provided.

1. stepbystep _____

2. porkchops _____

3. bed roll _____

4. merrygoround _____

5. seagull _____

6. dug out _____

Listen to your teacher say each word. Write the word on the line.

1. _____

2. _____

3. _____

Overview Silent Letter Words

Directions and Sample Answers for Activity Pages

Day 1	See "Model Silent Letter Words" below.
Day 2	Read the title and directions aloud. Invite students to divide each silent letter word into syllables using open and closed syllable patterns. (**writ/ten, wrin/kle, knap/sack, knick/ers, de/sign, gnash/ing, rhu/barb, rhi/zome**) Have students read each word and choose three words to use in sentences.
Day 3	Read the title and directions aloud. Invite students to sort words into silent letter word groups: **wr, kn, gn,** and **rh.** (**wr: wry, wring, wrench; kn: knob, knoll, kneeling; gn: gnarl, gnaw, gnat; rh: rhyme, rhea, rhino**) Have students choose two unknown words and define them using a dictionary.
Day 4	Read the title and directions aloud. Invite students to unscramble the sentences and write them on the lines. Then have students draw a picture that shows what is happening in each sentence. Have students read each sentence to a partner. (My baby sister wrote on the wall. Books are full of knowledge. My favorite food is gnocchi. A rhombus is different from a square.)
Day 5	Read the directions aloud. Allow time for students to complete the first task. (**wrig/gle, knap/sack, re/sign, rhi/no**). Next, pronounce the words **wrinkle, knotty, design,** and **rhea** and ask students to write them on the lines. Afterward, meet individually with students. Ask them to read each word on the assessment page. Discuss their results. Use their responses to plan further instruction and review.

Model Silent Letter Words

◆ Hand out the Day 1 activity page.

◆ Write **wrap** on the board and circle the **w. Say:** *Certain words have silent letters. In this word, the letter **w** is silent when it appears before **r**.*

◆ Write **wrapper** on the board. **Say:** *I will circle the **a** and **e**. I know double letter words are divided between the letters so I'll divide this word between the double **p**. (**wrap/per**) Copy what I did on your paper.*

◆ **Say:** *Now I want to read **wrapper**. The first syllable is closed, so it should make the short **a** sound. I'll try that first. I also know that the **w** is silent when it appears before **r**, so I won't make the **w** sound. I'll begin the word with the /**r**/ sound. The second syllable is also closed, but it is **r**-controlled. It makes the same sound as in **germ**. Model reading the two parts of the word and blending them together: /**rap**/ /**pûr**/.*

◆ **Say:** *Let's look at other words that have a silent letter. Repeat with **knotty, resign,** and **rhinestone**. (**knot/ty, re/sign, rhine/stone**) Explain that **k** and **g** are silent before **n**, and **h** is silent following **r**. Identify syllables as open or closed. Model reading the words. /**nŏt**/ /**tē**/, /**rē**/ /**zīn**/, and /**rīn**/ /**stōn**/*

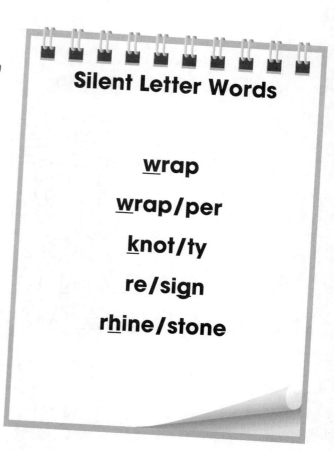

Silent Letter Words

<u>w</u>rap

<u>w</u>rap/per

<u>k</u>not/ty

re/si<u>g</u>n

r<u>h</u>ine/stone

Divide the following words into syllables. Underline the silent letter in each word.

wrap

wrapper

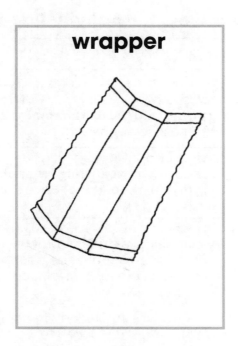

knotty

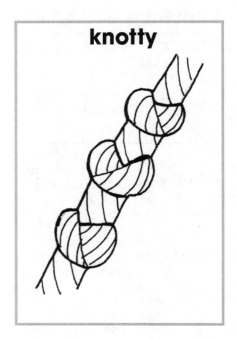

_____   _____   _____

resign

rhinestone

_____   _____

Words Divided

Look at the following words. Divide each silent letter word into syllables using open and closed syllables. Then read the words to a partner.

List 1:	List 2:	List 3:	List 4:
written	knapsack	design	rhubarb
wrinkle	knickers	gnashing	rhizome

Choose three words. Use each word in a sentence.

1. _____

_____

2. _____

_____

3. _____

_____

Silent Letter Word Sort

Sort the following silent letter words into groups. Share your results with a partner.

gnarl	rhea	gnat	rhino
kneeling	knob	rhyme	gnaw
wrench	knoll	wry	wring

wr	kn	gn	rh

Use a dictionary to define two words that you do not know. Write the definitions on the lines below.

1. _____

_____

2. _____

_____

Name _____

Sentence Scramble

Unscramble the sentences and write them on the lines. Then draw a picture that shows what is happening in each sentence. Read your sentences to a partner.

sister My wrote wall baby on the

_____

_____

_____

are Books knowledge of full

_____

_____

_____

food is gnocchi favorite My

_____

_____

square A is rhombus different a from

_____

_____

Assessment

Divide the following words into syllables.

wriggle

knapsack

resign

rhino

Listen to your teacher say each word. Write the word on the line.

1. _____

2. _____

3. _____

4. _____

Overview Contractions

Directions and Sample Answers for Activity Pages

Day 1	See "Model Contractions" below.
Day 2	Read the title and directions aloud. Invite students to draw a line from the word pairs to the contractions. (**will not-won't**; **we are-we're**; **I have-I've**; **she would-she'd**; **could not-couldn't**; **I will-I'll**; **are not-aren't**; **we have-we've**; **has not-hasn't**; **I am-I'm**; **he had-he'd**; **I had-I'd**) Have students read each contraction and choose three contractions to use in sentences.
Day 3	Read the title and directions aloud. Invite students to locate the ten contractions in the invitation. Then write the word pair for each contraction. Have students read each word to a partner. (**We're-we are**; **We'd-we would**; **you'd-you would**; **It's-it is**; **doesn't-does not**; **don't-do not**; **We're-we are**; **don't-do not**; **It's-it is**; **you'll-you will**)
Day 4	Read the title and directions aloud. Invite students to sort the contractions into six groups: are, have, is/has, not, will, had/would. Have students share results with a partner. (**are**: **they're**, **we're**; **have**: **could've**, **might've**; **is/has**: **where's who's**; **not**: **mustn't**, **wouldn't**; **will**: **that'll**, **you'll**; **had/would**: **they'd**, **you'd**)
Day 5	Read the directions aloud. Allow time for students to complete the first task. (**they're**, **they'd**, **might've**, **where's**, **that'll**). Next, pronounce the words **aren't**, **isn't**, **we'd**, and **we've** and ask students to write them on the lines. Afterward, meet individually with students. Ask them to read each word on the assessment page. Discuss their results. Use their responses to plan further instruction and review.

Model Contractions

◆ Hand out the Day 1 activity page.

◆ Write the words **you are** and **you're** on the board. **Say:** *A contraction is a short form of two words. One or more words is replaced by an apostrophe. Notice how I made **you are** into **you're**. I removed the **a** and replaced it with an apostrophe. You can make contractions out of many words.*

◆ Write the following sentence on the board: He cannot play outside because he is grounded. **Say:** *I can make **cannot** and **he is** into contractions.* Write **can't** and **he's** under the respective words. **Say:** *For **cannot**, I removed **no** and replaced them with an apostrophe. For **he is**, I removed **i** in **is** and replaced it with an apostrophe. Copy what I did on your paper.*

◆ Repeat with **should not**, **would not**, **he would**, **she is**, and **she has**.

Contractions

you + are = you're

cannot = can't

he + is = he's

should + not = shouldn't

would + not = wouldn't

he + would = he'd

she + is = she's

she + has = she's

Name _____

Write the contractions for the following pairs.

1. you are   _____

2. cannot   _____

3. he is   _____

4. should not   _____

5. would not   _____

6. he would   _____

7. she is   _____

8. she has   _____

Contraction Action

Look at the following words. Draw a line to match the word pairs to the correct contraction.

will not	he'd
we are	couldn't
I have	I'm
she would	we've
could not	I'll
I will	hasn't
are not	I'd
we have	won't
has not	we're
I am	aren't
he had	I've
I had	she'd

Choose three contractions to use in sentences.

1. _____

_____

2. _____

_____

3. _____

_____

RSVP

Read the invitation. Locate the ten contractions and write them at the bottom of the page. Then write the word pair for each contraction. Share your results with a partner.

Dear Aunt Alice,

We're having a party for Mom on Friday. We'd really like it if you'd be able to come. It's at 6:00 p.m. at our house. Mom doesn't know anything about the party, so make sure you don't tell her about it. We want her to be surprised. We're having her favorite food, but you don't have to bring anything. It's all taken care of. Let us know if you'll be able to come.

Love,
Rita and Sammy

Contraction   **Word Pairs**

_____   _____ and _____

_____   _____ and _____

_____   _____ and _____

_____   _____ and _____

_____   _____ and _____

_____   _____ and _____

_____   _____ and _____

_____   _____ and _____

_____   _____ and _____

_____   _____ and _____

Contraction Sort

Sort the following contractions into groups. Share your results with a partner.

where's	they'd	wouldn't	might've
mustn't	they're	you'd	who's
that'll	could've	you'll	we're

are	have	is/has	not	will	had/ would

Name _____

Assessment

Read the following word pairs. Write their contractions on the lines provided.

they are _____

they would _____

might have _____

where is _____

that will _____

Listen to your teacher say each word. Write the word on the line.

1. _____

2. _____

3. _____

4. _____

Overview Regular and Irregular Plurals

Directions and Sample Answers for Activity Pages

Day 1	See "Model Regular and Irregular Plurals" below.
Day 2	Read the title and directions aloud. Invite students to write the regular plural for each singular noun. Have students read each word to a partner and then choose three words to use in sentences. (**sponges, scripts, blades, lunches, taxes, glasses, buddies, flies, armies**)
Day 3	Read the title and directions aloud. Invite students to write the irregular plural for each singular noun. Have students read each word to a partner and then choose three words to use in sentences. (**dice, cacti, men, lives, wives, wolves, deer, dozen, sheep**)
Day 4	Read the title and directions aloud. Invite students to locate regular and irregular plural words in the word search.
Day 5	Read the directions aloud. Allow time for students to complete the first task. (**dolphins, gases, candies, cacti, leaves, moose**). Next, pronounce the words **blades, ditches, flies, lice, shelves,** and **deer** and ask students to write them on the lines. Afterward, meet individually with students. Ask them to read each word on the assessment page. Discuss their results. Use their responses to plan further instruction and review.

Model Regular and Irregular Plurals

◆ Hand out the Day 1 activity page. Then write the words **dog, fox,** and **berry** on the board. Write the letters **s, ch, sh,** and **x** in parentheses next to **fox**.

◆ **Say:** *Plural means more than one thing. There are many ways to make plurals. Look at the words on the board. Most nouns are made plural by simply adding an -s: the plural of **dog** is **dogs** .*Write **dogs** beside **dog**. **Say:** *Words ending in **s, ch, sh,** and **x**, like the word **fox** need an -es to make the plural form, like **foxes**.* Write **foxes** beside **fox**. **Say:** *For words ending in -y, drop the -y and add -ies: like **berry** becomes **berries**.* Write **berries** beside **berry**.

◆ Repeat with **cake, dish,** and **baby**.

◆ Write the words **woman, knife,** and **fish**.

◆ **Say:** *Some plural words don't follow the -s, -es, -ies pattern. These plurals are called irregular plurals. Look at **woman**. It becomes **women**.* Write **women** next to **woman**. **Say:** *Look at **knife**. We drop the -fe and add -ves.* Write **knives** next to **knife**. **Say:** *Now look at **fish**. Some plural words are exactly the same as their singular form. One **fish**, two **fish**, not **fishes**.* Write **fish** beside **fish**. **Say:** *Since irregular plurals do not follow rules, they must be memorized.*

◆ Repeat with **louse, shelf,** and **moose**.

Regular and Irregular Plurals

regular	irregular
dogs	women
foxes	knives
berries	fish
cakes	lice
dishes	shelves
babies	moose

Name _____

Write plurals for each word below.

Regular Plurals

1. cake _____
2. dish _____
3. baby _____

_____   _____

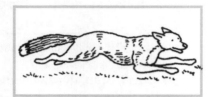

_____   _____

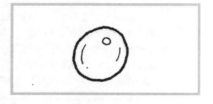

_____   _____

Irregular Plurals

1. louse _____
2. shelf _____
3. moose _____

_____   _____

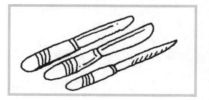

_____   _____

_____   _____

Follow the Rule

**Look at the following singular nouns. For each word, write the regular plural form.
Read each plural word to a partner.**

List 1:

sponge _____

script _____

blade _____

List 2:

lunch _____

tax _____

glass _____

List 3:

buddy _____

fly _____

army _____

Choose three words. Use each word in a sentence.

1. _____

_____

2. _____

_____

3. _____

_____

Remember It!

Look at the following singular nouns. For each word, write the irregular plural form.

List 1:	List 2:	List 3:
die _____	life _____	deer _____
cactus _____	wife _____	dozen _____
man _____	wolf _____	sheep _____

Choose three words. Use each word in a sentence.

1. _____

_____

2. _____

_____

3. _____

_____

Plural Word Search

Locate regular and irregular plural words in the word search.

Regular Plurals

bills	passes
peas	fries
forks	buddies

Irregular Plurals

geese	loaves
lice	deer
halves	moose

```
y  p  n  h  g  s  l  l  i  b
p  v  a  j  n  j  o  i  z  u
m  o  o  s  e  w  a  c  h  d
f  o  r  k  s  s  v  e  a  d
s  g  e  e  s  e  e  m  l  i
i  o  v  l  c  i  s  a  v  e
e  q  d  e  e  r  f  q  e  s
s  a  e  p  t  f  d  e  s  s
```

Assessment

Read the following singular nouns. Write their plurals on the lines provided.

dolphin _____

gas _____

candy _____

cactus _____

leaf _____

moose _____

Listen to your teacher say each word. Write the word on the line.

1. _____   4. _____

2. _____   5. _____

3. _____   6. _____

Overview· -ing and -ed Word Endings

Directions and Sample Answers for Activity Pages

Day 1	See "Model -ing and -ed Word Endings" below.
Day 2	Read the title and directions aloud. Invite students to divide each **-ing** and **-ed** word into syllables using closed syllable patterns. (**kick/ing, ask/ing, writ/ing, jok/ing, pet/ting, spot/ting, grunt/ed, act/ed, glid/ed, grad/ed, bud/ded, mat/ted**) Have students read each word and choose three words to use in sentences.
Day 3	Read the title and directions aloud. Invite students to sort the words into three groups: add **-ing**, drop **-e**, and add **-ing**, add double consonant **+ -ing**. (add **-ing**: **crying, swaying, draining**; drop **-e** and **-ing**: **scheming, dazing, boning**; add double consonant **+ -ing**: **planning, plodding, trotting**) Have students choose two unknown words and define them using a dictionary.
Day 4	Read the title and directions aloud. Invite students to sort the words into three groups: add **-ed**, add **-d**, double consonant **+ -ed**. (add **-ed**: **hinted, sculpted, quilted**; add **-d**: **fumed, used, robed**; double consonant + **-ed**: **snagged, nabbed, jutted**) Have students choose two unknown words and define them using a dictionary.
Day 5	Read the directions aloud. Allow time for students to complete the first task. (**melt/ing, not/ing, fit/ting, fund/ed, quot/ed, dot/ted**). Next, pronounce the words **kicking, joking, petting, hinted, used**, and **snagged** and ask students to write them on the lines. Afterward, meet individually with students. Ask them to read each word on the assessment page. Discuss their results. Use their responses to plan further instruction and review.

Model -ing and -ed Word Endings

◆ Hand out the Day 1 activity page. Copy the chart from the Day 1 activity page on the board.

◆ Write the following sentences on the board:
Is he playing baseball in the park?
I played there last Saturday.

◆ **Say:** *The first sentence talks about an action happening right now. The second sentence talks about an action that happened in the past.*

◆ Circle the root word in the verbs **playing** and **played**. **Say:** *By adding the endings -ing and -ed, we can change the meaning of any root word.* Have students write **playing** and **played** in the correct columns on the chart. Have students circle **play** in each word. Point out that **playing** has two syllables and **played** has one syllable.

◆ Repeat with **add**. (**adding, added**) Add each word to the chart, and point out that both words have two syllables.

◆ Write **fading** and **faded** on the chart. **Say:** *Adding -ing and -ed to verbs ending in silent e is different. The silent e is dropped before adding -ing or -ed.* Point out that both words have two syllables.

◆ Repeat with **rake, stop, skid**. Point out that when a word ends in a consonant, the consonant is often doubled.

-ing and -ed Word Endings

root	-ing	-ed
play	playing	played
add	adding	added
fade	fading	faded
rake	raking	raked
stop	stopping	stopped
skid	skidding	skidded

Add *-ing* and *-ed* endings to the words in the chart below.

Is he playing baseball in the park?

I played there last Saturday.

Root Word	-ing	-ed
play		
add		
fade		
rake		
stop		
skid		

Words Divided

Look at the following words. Divide each *-ing* and *-ed* word into syllables using closed syllable patterns. Then read the words to a partner.

List 1:	List 2:
kicking	grunted
asking	acted
writing	glided
joking	graded
petting	budded
spotting	matted

Choose three words. Use each word in a sentence.

1. _____

_____

2. _____

_____

3. _____

_____

-ing Word Sort

Sort the following *-ing* words into three groups. Share your results with a partner.

planning	dazing	swaying
crying	trotting	scheming
draining	boning	plodding

add -ing	drop -e and add -ing	double consonant + -ing

Use a dictionary to define two words that you do not know. Write the definitions on the lines below.

1. _____

_____

2. _____

_____

-ed Word Sort

Sort the following *-ed* words into three groups. Share your results with a partner.

fumed	hinted	quilted
sculpted	robed	jutted
snagged	nabbed	used

add -ed	add -d	double consonant + -ed

Use a dictionary to define two words that you do not know. Write the definitions on the lines below.

1. _____

_____

2. _____

_____

Assessment

Divide the following words into syllables.

melting _____

noting _____

fitting _____

funded _____

quoted _____

dotted _____

Listen to your teacher say each word. Write the word on the line.

1. _____

2. _____

3. _____

4. _____

5. _____

6. _____

Overview -er and -or Word Endings

Directions and Sample Answers for Activity Pages

Day 1	See "Model -er and -or Word Endings" below.
Day 2	Read the title and directions aloud. Invite students to divide each **-er** and **-or** word into syllables using open and closed syllable patterns. (**box/er, catch/er, clos/er, mak/er, log/ger, rob/ber, act/or, vis/it/tor, sen/a/tor, op/er/a/tor**) Have students read each word and choose three words to use in sentences.
Day 3	Read the title and directions aloud. Invite students to sort **-er** words into groups: add **-er**, drop **-e** and add **-er**, add double consonant + **-er**. (add **-er**: **player, fryer, blocker**; drop **-e** and add **-er**: **ruler, filer, timer**; add double consonant + **-er**: **swimmer, stopper, jogger**) Have students illustrate three words.
Day 4	Read the title and directions aloud. Invite students to sort **-or** words into groups: add **-or**, drop **-e** and add **-or**. (add **-or**: **visitor, sculptor, sailor**; drop **-e** and add **-or**: **survivor, illustrator, operator**) Have students illustrate three words.
Day 5	Read the directions aloud. Allow time for students to complete the first task. (**farm/er, vot/er, run/ner, sail/or, sen/a/tor**). Next, pronounce the words **player, writer, jogger, actor,** and **creator** and ask students to write them on the lines. Afterward, meet individually with students. Ask them to read each word on the assessment page. Discuss their results. Use their responses to plan further instruction and review.

Model -er and -or Word Endings

◆ Hand out the Day 1 activity page.

◆ Write the word **write** on the board.

◆ **Say:** *The word **write** is an action word, or verb. I can change this verb to a noun by adding **-er** to the end. Now the one-syllable word **write** becomes the two-syllable word **writer**. Notice how I dropped the final **-e** before adding the **-er**.*

◆ Repeat with **paint** and **swim**. (**painter, swimmer**) Point out that **painter** adds an **-er**, and **swimmer** adds a consonant **+ -er**. Both words are two syllables.

◆ Write **create** on the board. **Say:** *We add **-or** instead of **-er** to some words. There is no rule for this and you must memorize the spellings of these words. Write* **creator** *next to* **create**. **Say:** *Notice how I dropped the final **-e** before adding **-or**.*

◆ Repeat with **direct**. (**director**) Point out that **director** adds an **-or** and has three syllables.

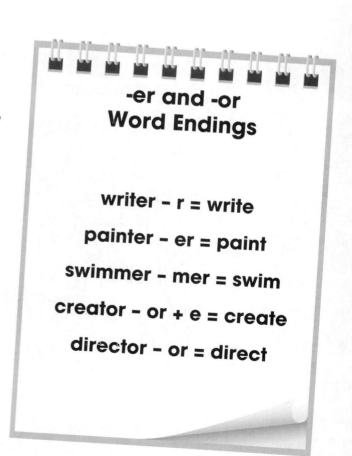

**-er and -or
Word Endings**

writer − r = write

painter − er = paint

swimmer − mer = swim

creator − or + e = create

director − or = direct

Look at the following words. What action word is the root word for each one?

writer

_____

painter

_____

swimmer

_____

creator

_____

director

_____

Words Divided

Look at the following words. Divide each *-er* and *-or* word into syllables using closed and open syllable patterns. Then read the words to a partner.

List 1:	List 2:
boxer	actor
catcher	visitor
closer	senator
maker	operator
logger	
robber	

Choose three words. Use each word in a sentence.

1. _____

_____

2. _____

_____

3. _____

_____

Name _____

-er Word Sort

Sort the following *-er* words into three groups. Share your results with a partner.

ruler	stopper	timer
jogger	player	fryer
blocker	filer	swimmer

add -er	drop -e and add -er	double consonant + -er

Draw illustrations of three *-er* words in the blank space below.

-or Word Sort

Sort the following *-or* words into two groups. Share your results with a partner.

visitor	illustrator	operator
survivor	sculptor	sailor

add -or	drop -e and add -or

Draw illustrations of three *-or* words in the blank space below.

Assessment

Divide the following words into syllables.

farmer   _____

voter   _____

runner   _____

sailor   _____

senator   _____

Listen to your teacher say each word. Write the word on the line.

1. _____

2. _____

3. _____

4. _____

5. _____

Overview Comparatives

Directions and Sample Answers for Activity Pages

Day 1	See "Model Comparatives" below.
Day 2	Read the title and directions aloud. Invite students to divide each **-er** and **-est** comparative word into syllables using open and closed syllable patterns. (**dark/er, dark/est, fast/er, fast/est; saf/er, saf/est, wid/er, wid/est; big/ger, big/gest, hot/ter, hot/test; sil/li/er, sil/li/est, sun/ni/er, sun/ni/est**) Have students read each word and choose three words to use in sentences.
Day 3	Read the title and directions aloud. Invite students to sort **-er** and **-est** comparative words into groups: add **-er/-est**, drop **-e** and add **-er/-est**, add double consonant **+ -er/-est**, drop **-y** and add **-ier/-iest**. (add **-er/-est**: **loudest, older, shortest**; drop **-e** and add **-er/-est**: **rudest, cuter, nicer**; add double consonant **+ -er/-est**: **hotter, biggest, saddest**; drop **-y** and add **-ier/-iest**: **fluffier, shiniest, prettier**) Have students illustrate three words.
Day 4	Read the title and directions aloud. Invite students to fill in the blanks using **-er** and **-est** comparative words. (**bigger, biggest; louder, loudest; higher, highest; smaller, smallest; grumpier, grumpiest; faster, fastest; wider, widest; shinier, shiniest; nicer, nicest**)
Day 5	Read the directions aloud. Allow time for students to complete the first task. (**short/er, short/est, tam/er, tam/est, mad/der, mad/dest, ear/li/er, ear/li/est**). Next, pronounce the words **darkest, nicer, hotter,** and **funniest** and ask students to write them on the lines. Afterward, meet individually with students. Ask them to read each word on the assessment page. Discuss their results. Use their responses to plan further instruction and review.

Model Comparatives

◆ Hand out the Day 1 activity page.

◆ Write **long, longer,** and **longest** on the board. Show students two pens of different lengths. Ask them which pen is **longer**. Add another pen of a different length and ask which pen is now the **longest**.

◆ Say: *We use an **-er** ending when we want to compare two things. We use an **-est** ending when we want to compare three things.*

◆ Show students how to divide these words into syllables. (**long/er, long/est**) Have students copy what you did on the activity page.

◆ Say: *For words that already end in **silent e**, drop the **silent e** and add **-er**.* Show students how to divide these words into syllables. (**nic/er, nic/est**)

◆ Repeat with **sad** (for closed syllable words that end in one consonant, double the consonant and add **-er** or **-est**), and **handy** (for words that end in **-y**, drop the **-y** and add **-ier** or **-iest**).

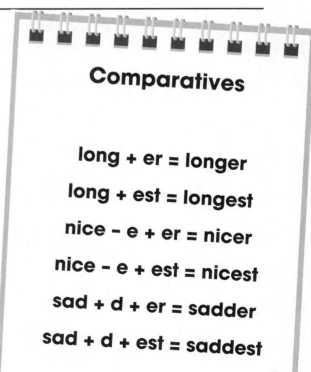

Comparatives

long + er = longer

long + est = longest

nice – e + er = nicer

nice – e + est = nicest

sad + d + er = sadder

sad + d + est = saddest

Add *-er* and *-est* endings to the words below.

Base Word	Base Word + -er	Base Word + -est
long	_____	_____
nice	_____	_____
sad	_____	_____
handy	_____	_____

Words Divided

Look at the following comparative words. Divide words into two or three syllables using closed and open syllable patterns. Then read the words to a partner.

List 1:	List 2:	List 3:	List 4:
darker	safer	bigger	sillier
darkest	safest	biggest	silliest
faster	wider	hotter	sunnier
fastest	widest	hottest	sunniest

Choose three words. Use each word in a sentence.

1. _____

_____

2. _____

_____

3. _____

_____

Comparative Word Sort

Sort the following comparative words into four groups. Illustrate the meaning of three words at the bottom of the page. Share your results with a partner.

rudest	hotter	older	prettier
fluffier	loudest	shiniest	nicer
biggest	cuter	shortest	saddest

add -er/-est	drop -e and add -er/-est	double consonant + -er/-est	drop -y and add -ier/-iest

Fill in the Blank

Fill in the blank with the correct comparative word. Share your results with a partner.

A dog is big, a horse is _____, but an elephant is
_____ of all.

A car is loud, a truck is _____, but an airplane is
_____ of all.

The gate is high, the house is _____, but the tree is
_____ of all.

A boy is small, a cat is _____, but the snail is
_____ of all.

My brother is grumpy, my mother is _____, but my father is
_____ of all.

A bike is fast, a car is _____, but a rocket is _____
of all.

The sidewalk is wide, the street is _____, but the bridge is
_____ of all.

A soup can is shiny, a new penny is _____, but a diamond is
_____ of all.

My mother is nice, my teacher is _____, but my grandmother is
_____ of all.

Assessment

Divide the following words into syllables.

shorter

shortest

tamer

tamest

madder

maddest

earlier

earliest

Listen to your teacher say each word. Write the word on the line.

1. _____

2. _____

3. _____

4. _____

Overview -y and -ly Word Endings

Directions and Sample Answers for Activity Pages

Day 1	See "Model -y and -ly Word Endings" below.
Day 2	Read the title and directions aloud. Invite students to sort **-y** words into two groups: add **-y** or drop **-e** and add **-y**. (add **-y**: **gloomy**, **leaky**, **thirsty**, **minty**; drop **-e** and add **-y**: **crazy**, **nosy**, **easy**, **slimy**) Have students illustrate three words.
Day 3	Read the title and directions aloud. Invite students to sort **-ly** words into two groups: add **-ly** or drop **-y** and add **-ily**. (add **-ly**: **bitterly**, **normally**, **strangely**, **creatively**; drop **-y** and add **-ily**: **happily**, **cozily**, **luckily**, **messily**) Have students illustrate three words.
Day 4	Read the title and directions aloud for both activities. Invite students to illustrate **-y** ending words. Invite students to draw a line from **-ly** words on the left to opposite **-ly** words on the right. (**deeply–shallowly**, **quietly–loudly**, **widely–narrowly**, **cleanly–messily**, **slowly–quickly**, **calmly–nervously**, **meanly–nicely**, **daily–nightly**)
Day 5	Read the directions aloud. Allow time for students to complete the first task. (**bloody**, **bouncy**, **finely**, **merrily**) Next, pronounce the words **grassy**, **slimy**, **deeply**, and **happily** and ask students to write them on the lines. Afterward, meet individually with students. Ask them to read each word on the assessment page. Discuss their results. Use their responses to plan further instruction and review.

Model -y and -ly Word Endings

◆ Hand out the Day 1 activity page.

◆ Write **grass** and **grassy** on the board.

◆ **Say:** *The base word of* **grassy** *is* **grass***, which is a noun that names something. When we add* **-y** *to the word* **grass***, we make a describing word, or adjective.* Provide examples that show how the word **grassy** can be used to describe something: a grassy field, a grassy hilltop. Have students complete the sentences on the activity page.

◆ Write **bubble** and **bubbly** on the board. **Say:** *When a word ends in silent* **e***, drop the* **-e** *before adding* **-y***.* Have students complete the sentences on the activity page.

◆ Write **bad** and **badly** on the board.

◆ **Say:** *The base word of* **badly** *is* **bad***, which is an adjective that describes something. When we add* **-ly** *to the word* **bad***, we make an adverb, which is a word that tells how something is done. Adverbs describe verbs, adjectives, and other adverbs.* Provide an example that shows how the word **badly** can be used to describe something: **he behaved badly**. Have students complete the sentences on the activity page.

◆ Write **angry** and **angrily** on the board. **Say:** *When a word ends in* **-y***, drop the* **-y** *and add* **-ily***.* Have students complete the sentences on the activity page.

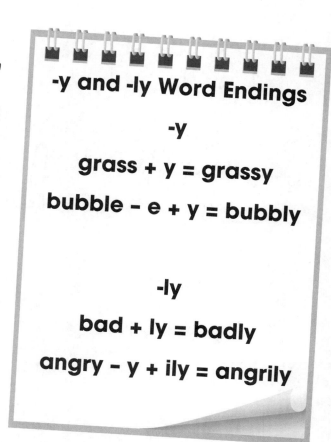

-y and -ly Word Endings

-y

grass + y = grassy

bubble − e + y = bubbly

-ly

bad + ly = badly

angry − y + ily = angrily

Look at each picture. Then complete the sentences.

This field has a lot of

_____.

This is a

_____ field.

The stew is full of

_____.

The _____
stew smells so good.

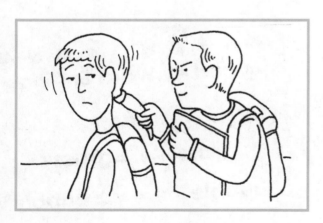

The boy is being

_____.

The boy is behaving

_____.

The girl is

_____.

The girl throws the
ball _____.

-y Word Sort

Sort the following -y words into two groups: add -y and drop -e add -y. Illustrate the meaning of three words at the bottom of the page. Share your results with a partner.

| slimy | nosy | gloomy | leaky |
| minty | thirsty | easy | crazy |

| **add -y** | **drop -e and and add -y** |

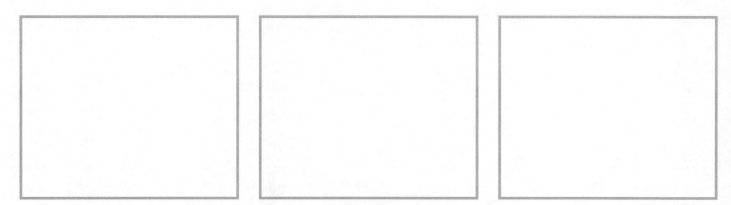

-ly Word Sort

Sort the following *-ly* words into two groups: add *-ly* and drop *-y* add *-ily*. Illustrate the meaning of three words at the bottom of the page. Share your results with a partner.

creatively	cozily	normally	strangely
happily	bitterly	messily	luckily

add -ly	drop -y add -ily

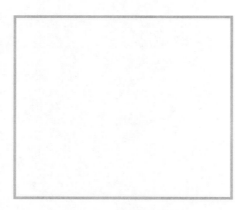

Drawing and Matching

Draw illustrations of the following -y word phrases:

　　a messy room　　　　　　　　a juicy fruit　　　　　　　a squeaky door

Draw a line from -ly words on the left to -ly words on the right that mean the opposite.

deeply	nicely
quietly	quickly
widely	nightly
cleanly	shallowly
slowly	nervously
calmly	narrowly
meanly	loudly
daily	messily

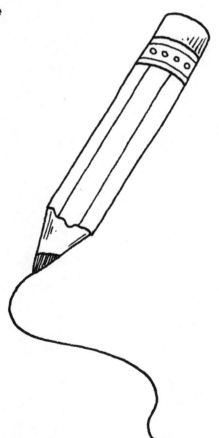

Assessment

Add -y to the following words.

blood _____

bounce _____

Add -ly to the following words.

fine _____

merry _____

Listen to your teacher say each word. Write the word on the line.

1. _____

2. _____

3. _____

4. _____

Overview Suffix -less

Directions and Sample Answers for Activity Pages

Day 1	See "Model Suffix -less" below.
Day 2	Read the title and directions aloud. Invite students to read each base word and suffix word. Then have students illustrate both words showing how the meaning of the base word changes when the suffix **-less** is added. Have students share illustrations with a partner.
Day 3	Read the title and directions aloud. Invite students to draw a line from the **-less** word on the left to the **un-** word on the right that has the same or about the same meaning. Have students choose four **-less** words and use them in sentences. (**careless-unthinking, fearless-unafraid, useless-unworthy, tasteless-unflavored, joyless-unhappy, motionless-unmoving, humorless-unfunny**)
Day 4	Read the title and directions aloud. Invite students to read the words in the box and match them to the correct definition. Then have students locate each **-less** word in the word search. (**shameless, tearless, useless, voiceless, dreamless, restless, treeless, homeless**)
Day 5	Read the directions aloud. Allow time for students to complete the first task. (**priceless, breathless, ownerless, nameless, defenseless, thoughtless**). Next, pronounce the words **cloudless, spotless, joyless,** and **careless** and ask students to write them on the lines. Afterward, meet individually with students. Ask them to read each word on the assessment page. Discuss their results. Use their responses to plan further instruction and review.

Model Suffix -less

◆ Hand out the Day 1 activity page.

◆ Write the following sentence on the board: Most spiders are harmless.

◆ **Say:** *A suffix is a group of letters at the end of a word that changes the meaning of the word. The suffix **-less** means "without." Listen to this sentence: Most spiders are harmless.* Circle **-less** in **harmless**. *The word **harmless** literally means "without harm," or "does no harm." So this sentence means that most spiders do not harm people. Copy what I did onto your paper.*

◆ Ask students to create new words on the activity page. (**weight/weightless, sleep/sleepless,** and **hope/hopeless**)

◆ Then ask students to write a sentence using each new word.

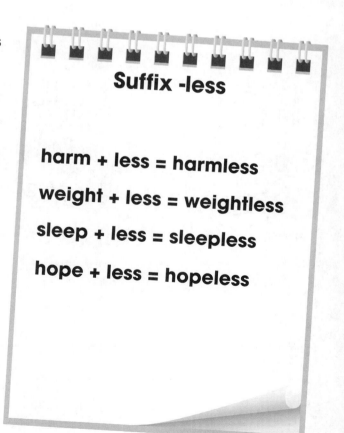

Suffix -less

harm + less = harmless

weight + less = weightless

sleep + less = sleepless

hope + less = hopeless

Suffix -less

Add *-less* to the following words. Then use the new word in a sentence.

 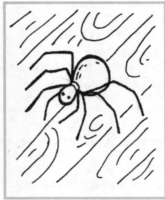

harm _____

_____

_____

weight _____

_____

_____

sleep _____

_____

_____

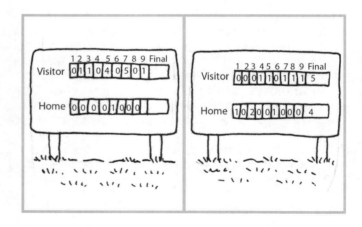

hope _____

_____

_____

Draw -less

Read each base word and suffix word. Draw illustrations that show how the meaning of each base word changes when the suffix *-less* is added. Share the illustrations with a partner.

Base Word

-less Word

power

cloud

fear

spot

powerless

cloudless

fearless

spotless

Suffix/Prefix Synonym Match

Draw a line from the *-less* word on the left to the *un-* word on the right that has the same or similar meaning.

careless   unmoving

fearless   unhappy

useless   unfunny

tasteless   unthinking

joyless   unflavored

motionless   unafraid

humorless   unworthy

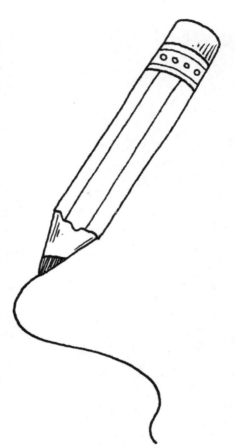

Choose four *-less* words and use them in sentences.

1. _____

_____

2. _____

_____

3. _____

_____

4. _____

_____

Word Search

Read the words in the box. Fill in the blanks with the correct words and then circle the words in the word search.

tearless	homeless	restless	treeless
dreamless	useless	voiceless	shameless

without shame: _____

without dreams: _____

without tears: _____

without rest: _____

without use: _____

without trees: _____

without a voice: _____

without a home: _____

```
t  w  s  s  e  l  m  a  e  r  d
r  e  j  a  c  l  e  d  d  b  l
e  b  a  h  o  m  e  l  e  s  s
e  a  d  r  m  a  w  f  v  h  s
l  d  e  x  l  p  g  s  f  f  e
e  j  s  u  s  e  l  e  s  s  l
s  a  s  z  v  g  s  o  o  q  t
s  q  i  t  e  d  d  s  w  p  s
f  v  o  i  c  e  l  e  s  s  e
s  s  e  l  e  m  a  h  s  j  r
```

Assessment

Read the following words. Add the suffix *-less* to each base word and write the new word on the line provided.

price   _____

breath   _____

owner   _____

name   _____

defense   _____

thought   _____

Listen to your teacher say each word. Write the word on the line.

1. _____

2. _____

3. _____

4. _____

Overview Suffix -ion, -sion, -tion

Directions and Sample Answers for Activity Pages

Day 1	See "Model Suffix -ion, -sion, -tion" below.
Day 2	Read the title and directions aloud. Invite students to divide each word into syllables using closed and open syllable patterns. (**cham/pi/on, ex/pres/sion, di/vi/sion, ad/mis/sion, def/i/ni/tion, des/crip/tion, con/di/tion, tra/di/tion**) Have students read each word and choose three words to use in sentences.
Day 3	Read the title and directions aloud. Invite students to sort words into the three groups: -ion, -sion, -tion. (**-ion: production, action, subtraction; -sion: permission, extension, decision; -tion: competition, exploration, starvation**) Have student choose three words and define them.
Day 4	Read the title and directions aloud. Invite students to read the narrative and identify the six -ion, -sion, and -tion words. Have students write the words on the lines provided. (**vacation, directions, station, question, confusion, action**)
Day 5	Read the directions aloud. Allow time for students to complete the first task. (**ex/cep/tion, re/la/tion, col/lec/tion, oc/ca/sion, vi/sion**). Next, pronounce the words **direction, explosion, addition,** and **definition** and ask students to write them on the lines. Afterward, meet individually with students. Ask them to read each word on the assessment page. Discuss their results. Use their responses to plan further instruction and review.

Model Suffix -ion, -sion, -tion

◆ Hand out the Day 1 activity page.

◆ Write **direct-direction, collide-collision**, and **confirm-confirmation** on the board and underline each suffix. **Say:** *The underlined parts of these words are called suffixes. Adding suffixes to a base word changes both the meaning and the part of speech.*

◆ Point out the changes in parts of speech: **direct** (verb), **direction** (noun), **collide** (verb), **collision** (noun), etc.

◆ **Say:** *What do you notice about how the base words change when suffixes are added?* Students should notice that **-ion** is added to **direct**, **-de** is dropped before adding **-sion** to **collision**, and **-ation** is added to **confirm**. **Say:** *Sometimes **-ion** is simply added as in* **direction**. *The base word **direct** already ends in a **t**. Other times, the base word changes before adding the **-sion** or **-tion**. Most of these words do not follow a rule, so they must be memorized.*

◆ Show students how to divide the suffix words into syllables using closed and open syllable patterns: (**di/rec/tion, col/li/sion, con/fir/ma/tion**). Have students copy what you did on the activity page.

◆ Repeat with **explode-explosion, add-addition,** and **explain-explanation**.

◆ Then write **region, caution,** and **mansion**. Underline **-ion, -tion,** and **-sion. Say:** *Sometimes **-ion, -tion,** and **-sion** end a word without a base-word beginning.*

Suffix
-ion, -sion, -tion

verb + -ion = noun

direct + ion = direction
collide – de + sion = collision
confirm + a + tion = confirmation
explode – de + sion = explosion
add + i + tion = addition
explain – in + na + tion = explanation

Suffix -ion, -sion, -tion

Write the part of speech for each word below.

Base Word	Part of Speech	Base Word + Suffix	Part of Speech
direct	_____	direction	_____
collide	_____	collision	_____
confirm	_____	confirmation	_____
explode	_____	explosion	_____
add	_____	addition	_____
explain	_____	explanation	_____
region	_____		
caution	_____		
mansion	_____		

Words Divided

Look at the following words. Use closed and open syllable patterns to divide each word into syllables. Then read the words to a partner.

List 1: -ion	List 2: -sion	List 3: -tion	List 4: no base word
champion	division	definition	condition
expression	admission	description	tradition

Choose three words. Use each word in a sentence.

1. _____

_____

2. _____

_____

3. _____

_____

Word Sort

Sort the following words into groups using suffixes *-ion*, *-sion*, and *-tion*. Share your results with a partner.

competition	decision	subtraction
production	action	extension
permission	exploration	starvation

-ion	-sion	-tion

Choose three words and write a definition on the lines below.

1. _____

_____

2. _____

_____

3. _____

_____

Are We There Yet?

Read the narrative. Identify the six *-ion*, *-sion*, and *-tion* words and write them on the lines provided.

Sam and his family were on vacation, looking for Beeds Lake. So far, they hadn't had much luck.

"Dad doesn't like to ask for directions, does he?" Sam whispered to his mother, who just smiled.

At a gas station, while Sam's father was filling up the van, Sam asked the manager a question.

"How do we get to Beeds Lake?"

The manager drew a map on the back of a napkin and gave it to Sam. When Sam got back in the van, his father was eating a sandwich.

"Here's a napkin for you, Dad," Sam said as he gave his father the napkin with the map on it.

Sam's father laughed. "I'm sorry for all the confusion, Sam. This map will help a lot."

Soon, Sam and his family were ready for action at Beeds Lake.

Assessment

Divide the following words into syllables using closed and open syllable patterns.

exception

relation

collection

occasion

vision

Listen to your teacher say each word. Write the word on the line.

1. _____

2. _____

3. _____

4. _____

Overview Greek Roots

Directions and Sample Answers for Activity Pages

Day 1	See "Model Greek Roots" below.
Day 2	Read the title and directions aloud. Invite students to use a dictionary to complete the chart and define the **-ology** words: **ecology** (*eco* = house): the study of living things and their environments; **geology** (*geo* = earth): the study of Earth; **zoology** (*zoo* = animals): the study of animals; **biology** (*bio* = life): the study of life; **meteorology** (*meteor* = lofty): the study of weather. Have students read each word and choose three words to use in sentences.
Day 3	Read the title and directions aloud. Invite students to sort words into the three groups: meter, scope, and tele. (**meter: speedometer, thermometer, centimeter, diameter; scope: kaleidoscope, periscope, microscope, stethoscope; tele: telecast, telegraph, telegram, telephone**) Have students choose four words and define them.
Day 4	Read the title and directions aloud. Invite students to fill in the blanks with the correct Greek root. Then locate each Greek root in the word search. (**self** = *auto*, **light** = *photo*, **heat** = *therm*, **measure** = *meter*, **life** = *bio*, **write** = *graph*, **animal** = *zoo*, **earth** = *geo*)
Day 5	Read the directions aloud. Allow time for students to complete the first task. (***tele*** = far, ***graph*** = write, ***meter*** = measure, ***scope*** = see, ***geo*** = earth) Next, pronounce the words **microscope, telephone, biology,** and **photograph** and ask students to write them on the lines. Afterward, meet individually with students. Ask them to read each word on the assessment page. Discuss their results. Use their responses to plan further instruction and review.

Model Greek Roots

◆ Hand out the Day 1 activity page.

◆ Write **biography, photograph, program,** and **telescope** on the board.

◆ **Say:** *Many English words have their beginnings from the Greek language. We say that these words are based on Greek roots. Understanding Greek roots helps you read unfamiliar words, especially in social studies, science, health, and math.*

◆ **Say:** *Look at the word **biography** on the board. This word is made of two Greek roots: **bio** and **graph**. **Bio** means "life" and **graph** means "to write." When you put the two Greek roots together and think about what they might mean, you see that **biography** means writing about someone's life.*

◆ **Say:** *Sometimes you cannot take the meaning of Greek roots literally. Look at **photograph**. **Photo** means "light" and we already know that **graph** means "to write." Does **photograph** mean "light write"? No. That doesn't make sense. We need to think about "to write" in a different way. **Write** means making a picture using words. So **photograph** means making a picture with light. Copy what I did onto your paper.*

◆ Repeat with **program** and **microscope**. (***pro* = before, *gram* = something written; *tele* = far, *scope* = to see**)

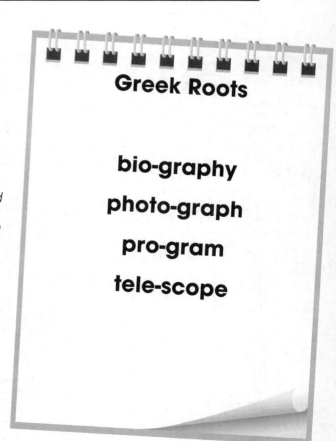

Greek Roots

bio-graphy

photo-graph

pro-gram

tele-scope

Name _____

Greek Roots

List the Greek roots for each word. Then use the meaning of each root to write a definition.

English Word	Greek Roots/ Meanings	Definition
biography	_____ _____	_____ _____
photograph	_____	_____
program	_____ _____	_____ _____
telescope	_____ _____	_____ _____

-ology Words

Look at the words in the chart below. They end in the Greek root *-ology*, which means "the study of." Use a dictionary to complete the chart.

English Word	Greek Root/Meaning	English Definition
ecology	_____	the study of _____
geology	_____	the study of _____
zoology	_____	the study of _____
biology	_____	the study of _____
meteorology	_____	the study of _____

Choose three *-ology* words to use in sentences.

1. _____

_____

2. _____

_____

3. _____

_____

Greek Root Word Sort

The following words are based on three Greek roots: *meter*, which means "measure"; *scope*, which means "to see"; and *tele*, which means "far." Sort the words into the three groups.

telecast	periscope	microscope	stethoscope
speedometer	thermometer	centimeter	telephone
kaleidoscope	telegram	telegraph	diameter

meter	scope	tele

Choose four words and write a definition on the lines below.

1. _____

_____

2. _____

_____

3. _____

_____

4. _____

_____

Greek Roots Word Search

The Greek roots on the right match the English words on the left. Fill in the blanks with the correct Greek roots and then find each root in the word search.

self: _____

light: _____

heat: _____

measure: _____

life: _____

write: _____

animal: _____

earth: _____

auto	**meter**
bio	**photo**
geo	**therm**
graph	**zoo**

```
e  z  o  o  e  g  e  m  p
o  t  h  t  t  r  t  a  h
m  e  t  e  r  a  u  t  o
p  h  h  l  a  p  r  b  t
b  i  e  e  f  h  g  i  o
p  o  r  v  g  e  e  t  h
s  r  m  t  b  i  o  p  r
```

Assessment

Write the meaning of each Greek root on the lines provided.

tele _____

graph _____

meter _____

scope _____

geo _____

Listen to your teacher say each word. Write the word on the line.

1. _____

2. _____

3. _____

4. _____

Overview Latin Roots

Directions and Sample Answers for Activity Pages

Day 1	See "Model Latin Roots" below.
Day 2	Read the title and directions aloud. Invite students to use a dictionary to complete the chart and define the Latin words: **vista** = a distant view; **visionary** = a person who sees what things could be like; **supervisor** = a person who oversees a project or group of people; **invisible** = unable to be seen, hidden from view; **auditorium** = a large room where people sit to see and hear a performance; **audience** = a group of people who see and hear a performance; **auditory** = using the sense of hearing; **inaudible** = not being heard clearly, garbled. Have students read each word and choose two **vis** words and two **audi** words to use in sentences.
Day 3	Read the title and directions aloud. Invite students to sort words into the three groups: **scrib/script**, **pes/ped**, and **port**. (**scrib/script: describe, transcript, prescription; pes/ped: biped, moped, pedal; port: import, portable, support**) Have students choose three words and define them.
Day 4	Read the title and directions aloud. Invite students to fill in the blanks using Latin-based words. (**object, eruption, digit, nervous, inspector, construction, collar, flexible**)
Day 5	Read the directions aloud. Allow time for students to complete the first task. (**vis** = to see; **audi** = to hear; **trans** = across; **scrib** = to write, **ped** = foot) Next, pronounce the words **manuscript, vision, pedal,** and **transport** and ask students to write them on the lines. Afterward, meet individually with students. Ask them to read each word on the assessment page. Discuss their results. Use their responses to plan further instruction and review.

Model Latin Roots

Latin Roots

manuscript =
manu (hand) + script (to write)

subtract =
sub (under) + tract (pull away)

transport =
trans (across) + port (carry)

vision = vis (to see)

structure = struct (to build)

◆ Hand out the Day 1 activity page. Write **manuscript, subtract, vision, transport,** and **structure** on the board. **Say:** *Many English words come from the Latin language. These words are based on Latin roots. Understanding Latin roots helps you read unfamiliar words.*

◆ **Say:** *Look at the word **manuscript**. This word is made of two Latin roots: **manu** and **script**. Manu means "hand" and **script** means "to write." When you put the two Latin roots together, you see that **manuscript** means "writing by hand." We know that **manuscripts** can be written or typed by hand.*

◆ **Say:** *Sometimes you cannot take the meaning of Latin roots literally. Look at **subtract**. **Sub** means "below or lower" and **tract** means "to draw or pull." Does **subtract** mean draw below or pull under? Not quite. We need to think about both roots in different ways. In this word, **tract** means to take away and **sub** means under. So **subtract** means to take away from underneath, as in a subtraction problem.*

◆ Repeat with **transport**. (**trans = across, port = to carry**)

◆ **Say:** *Sometimes just one Latin root makes a word such as **vision** (**vis** means "to see"), or **structure** (**struct** means "to build").*

Name _____

Latin Roots

List the Latin roots for each word. Then use the meaning of each root to write a definition.

English Word	Latin Roots	Root Meanings	Definition
manuscript			
subtract			
transport			
vision			
structure			

Related Roots vis and audi

Look at the following words in the chart below. They contain the Latin roots *vis* and *audi*. Use a dictionary to find out how *vis* means "to see" and *audi* means "to hear."

English Word	English Definition
vista	_____
visionary	_____
supervisor	_____
invisible	_____
auditorium	_____
audience	_____
auditory	_____
inaudible	_____

Choose two *vis* words and two *audi* words to use in sentences.

1. _____

_____

2. _____

_____

3. _____

_____

4. _____

_____

Latin Root Word Sort

The following words are based on three Latin roots: *scrib* or *script*, which means "to write"; *ped* or *pes*, which means "foot"; and *port*, which means "to carry." Sort the words into the three groups.

transcript	support	describe
import	prescription	moped
biped	pedal	portable

scrib/script	ped/pes	port

Choose three words and write a definition on the lines below.

1. _____

_____

2. _____

_____

3. _____

_____

Fill in the Blank

Read the Latin-based words in the box. Then fill in the blanks with the correct words. Share your results with a partner.

inspector	object	digit	flexible
eruption	construction	nervous	collar

What is that _____ flying in the sky? Is it a bird . . . a plane?

The volcanic _____ left the sky dark for weeks.

Another word for finger is _____.

I want to perform in the play, but I'm too _____ to try out for a part.

The _____ carefully reviewed all our paperwork.

The _____ crew worked day and night to finish the building on time.

You've got dirt on the _____ of your shirt.

A gymnast must be _____ enough to bend and twist in different ways.

Assessment

Write the meaning of each Latin root on the lines provided.

vis _____

audi _____

trans _____

scrib _____

ped _____

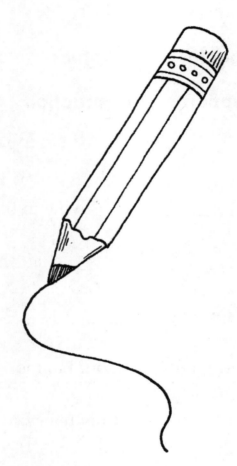

Listen to your teacher say each word. Write the word on the line.

1. _____

2. _____

3. _____

4. _____

Overview Homographs and Heteronyms

Directions and Sample Answers for Activity Pages

Day 1	See "Model Homographs and Heteronyms" below.
Day 2	Read the title and directions aloud. Invite students to read the homographs. Then have students illustrate two meanings for each word. Under each illustration, have students write a sentence that explains their artwork.
Day 3	Read the title and directions aloud. Invite students to illustrate the heteronym-based sentences. Have students share their word with a partner.
Day 4	Read the title and directions aloud. Invite students to sort words into the two groups: homographs and heteronyms (homographs: **lap**, **crow**, **lock**, **fan**, **bill**; heteronyms: **close**, **commune**, **record**, **refuse**, **wind**). Have student choose two homographs and illustrate two meanings. Have students choose one heteronym and include both uses of the word in the sentence.
Day 5	Read the directions aloud. Allow time for students to complete the first two tasks. (For example, **pen**: The pigs are in the pen. I use a pen to write with at school. **jam**: I like jam on my bread. We got in a terrible traffic jam on the highway. **dove**: The dove dove in the water to get the fish. **wound**: The wound on my arm finally healed after I wound gauze around it.) Next, pronounce the words **picture**, **crow**, **bass**, and **content** and ask students to write them on the lines. Afterward, meet individually with students. Ask them to read each word on the assessment page. Discuss their results. Use their responses to plan further instruction and review.

Model Homographs and Heteronyms

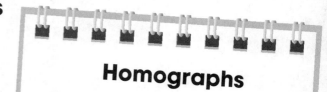

◆ Hand out the Day 1 activity page. Write each homograph sentence from the page on the board.

◆ **Say:** *Many words in our language are homographs. Homographs are words that are spelled the same but are different in meaning and in origin. Look at these sentences. What does the word **ball** mean in each one?*

◆ Discuss the meaning of **ball** in each sentence. 1. noun: a round object that you might throw in a game. 2. verb: the act of making something into a ball as in when you wind up cotton yarn (from the Middle English **bal**). 3. noun: meaning a fancy party or dance, from the French word **baler**, which means "to dance."

◆ Write the heteronym sentences on the board. **Say:** *Many homographs are also heteronyms. Heteronyms are words that are spelled the same but are pronounced differently and have a different meaning. In this first sentence, the word **minute** is a noun that means 60 seconds. It is pronounced /mĭ/ /nĭt/ with the emphasis on the first syllable. In the second sentence, **minute** is an adjective, and it means very small or tiny. It is pronounced /mī/ /nūt/ with the emphasis on the second syllable.*

Homographs

ball (noun): a round object that you throw

ball (verb): to make or roll something into a round, ball-like shape

ball (noun): a fancy party where people dance

Heteronyms

minute (noun): a unit of measurement for time equal to 60 seconds

minute (adjective): very small or tiny

Homographs and Heteronyms

Write the meaning, origin, and part of speech for each homograph and heteronym.

Homographs

Sentence	Meaning and Origin	Part of Speech
1. I threw the ball to first base.		
2. My mother and I ball cotton on rainy afternoons.		
3. The fairy princess went to the ball and danced with the handsome prince.		

Heteronyms

Sentence	Meaning and Part of Speech	Pronunciation
I'm leaving for school in one minute.		
My chances of winning are minute.		

Homographs Alive

Read the following homographs. Illustrate two meanings for each word. For example, for the word *match*, you could draw one illustration showing two matching pictures and a second illustration showing someone using a match to start a campfire. Under each illustration, write a sentence that explains your artwork.

1. band

2. picture

3. tick

I Bow With My Bow?

Read the following sentences containing heteronyms. Illustrate the sentences. Think carefully as heteronyms can be tricky. Share your work with a partner.

1. My bass /băs/ fish plays the bass /bās/.

2. Before signing the Mayflower Compact /kom/ /pact/, the Pilgrims were very compact /kuhm/ /pakt/ on the ship.

3. I shed many tears /teerz/ when I saw the tears /tairz/ on my shirt.

4. I was very content /kuhn/ /tent/ with the content /kon/ /tent/ of my book report.

5. I couldn't console /kuhn/ /sōl/ my sister after she broke her stereo console /kŏn/ /sōl/.

6. I signed a contract /kon/ /tract/ saying I would probably not contract /kuhm/ /tract/ the flu. It didn't work.

Homograph and Heteronym Word Sort

Read the following words and sort them into two groups: homographs and heteronyms. Share your work with a partner.

lap	record	wind	commune	bill
close	lock	fan	crow	refuse

Homographs	**Heteronyms**

Choose two homographs and illustrate at least two meanings for each word. Label each illustration with the homograph you used.

Choose one heteronym and include both uses of the word in one sentence. Refer to the Day 3 activity for help, if needed.

1. _____

_____

2. _____

Name _____

Assessment

Write two sentences that show two different meanings for each of the following homographs.

pen

jam

1. _____

2. _____

3. _____

4. _____

Write one sentence for each of the following heteronyms that includes both uses of the word.

dove

wound

1. _____

2. _____

Listen to your teacher say each word. Write the word on the line.

1. _____   **3.** _____

2. _____   **4.** _____

Overview Homophones

Directions and Sample Answers for Activity Pages

Day 1	See "Model Homophones" below.
Day 2	Read the title and directions aloud. Invite students to read the homophones and illustrate the meanings for each one. Then have students choose one homophone for each set and write a sentence that explains their illustration.
Day 3	Read the title and directions aloud. Invite students to read the homophones in both columns and draw a line matching the word from Column A with its homophone in Column B. Have students share their work with a partner. (**grease/Greece, days/daze, dense/dents, principle/principal, shear/sheer, board/bored, team/teem, pedal/peddle, muscle/mussel, wave/waive**)
Day 4	Read the title and directions aloud. Invite students to read the homophones in the box. Have students fill in the blanks for each sentence using the homophones. Have students share their work with a partner. (**teas, sow, dew, sees, sew, seize, due, tease, tees, seas, do, so**)
Day 5	Read the directions aloud. Allow time for students to complete the first task. (For example, **side**: I dented the left side of my toy truck. **sighed**: My teacher sighed when she saw our artwork. **stair**: To get to the gym, go down the stairs. **stare**: It's not nice to stare at people.) Next, read the following sentences and have students write the homophone on the lines provided. The lion's mane was golden in color. I want a toy that costs only 75 cents. It's not nice to tease people. What should I wear to school today? Afterward, meet individually with students. Ask them to read each word on the assessment page. Discuss their results. Use their responses to plan further instruction and review.

Model Homophones

◆ Hand out the Day 1 activity page. Then write **allowed** and **aloud** on the board.

◆ **Say:** *Many words in our language are homophones. Homophones are words that sound the same but have different spellings and meanings.* **Homophone** *is a word based on two Greek roots:* **homo,** *which means "same," and* **phone,** *which means "sound." So homophones are words with the same sound. Look at the two words on the board. These two words sound the same. Read the words. But they mean two different things and are spelled differently. Let's use these words in sentences.*

◆ Help students write a sentence for each word on the Day 1 activity page. For example, I wasn't **allowed** to play outside after dark. Please read **aloud** to the class. **Say:** *If I used the wrong spelling for these sentences, they wouldn't make sense.*

◆ Repeat with **hair/hare**, **heel/heal/he'll**, and **cents/scents/sense**.

◆ **Say:** *Sometimes homophones can be spelled three different ways and have three different meanings. If I used the wrong form of homophones in these sentences, they wouldn't make sense.*

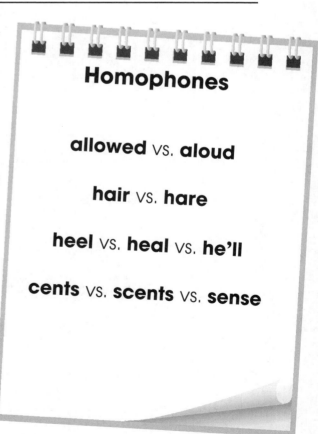

Homophones

allowed vs. **aloud**

hair vs. **hare**

heel vs. **heal** vs. **he'll**

cents vs. **scents** vs. **sense**

Name _____

Homophones

Read the following homophones. Then write sentences for each word.

allowed   **aloud**

hair   **hare**

_____   _____

_____   _____

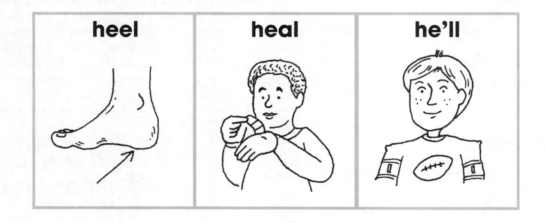

heel   **heal**   **he'll**

_____

_____

cents   **scents**   **sense**

_____

_____

Unit 22 • Everyday Phonics Intervention Activities Grade 5 • © Newmark Learning, LLC

Homophones

Read the following homophones. Illustrate the different meanings for each homophone. Choose one homophone and write a sentence on the lines provided that explains your illustration. Share your results with a partner.

1. horse	hoarse

_____

_____

2. cymbal	symbol

_____

_____

3. main	Maine	mane

_____

_____

4. ware	wear	where

_____

_____

Name _____

...ne Match

... homophones in both columns. For each word in Column A there is a matching
... phone in Column B. Draw a line connecting the homophones. Share your work with
... partner.

Column A	Column B
grease	bored
days	mussel
dense	waive
principle	teem
shear	daze
board	principal
team	sheer
pedal	dents
muscle	Greece
wave	peddle

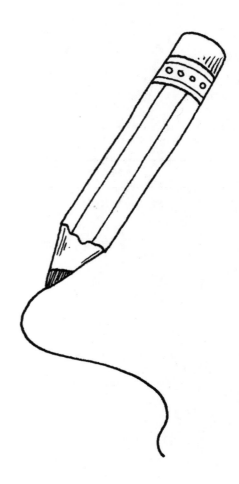

Which Is Which?

Read the following homophones. Complete each sentence with the correct homophone. Share your work with a partner.

Homophone Word List

sees	**dew**	**teas**	**sew**
seas	**do**	**tease**	**so**
seize	**due**	**tees**	**sow**

I enjoy drinking flavored _____ from other countries.

Farmers _____ their fields with seeds.

Moisture on the morning grass is called _____.

The bird _____ a worm in the dirt. Poor worm.

My grandmother knows how to _____ my doll's clothes.

Pirates _____ treasure from other ships.

The _____ date for my library book is this Saturday.

When I _____ my little brother, I get in a lot of trouble.

Golf balls sit on top of _____ before they are hit.

I love sailing on the high _____.

What did you _____ last night?

I got straight As, _____ I get a pizza party.

Name _____

nt

sentences that show the two meanings for the following homophones.

side/sighed

1. _____

_____

2. _____

_____

stair/stare

1. _____

_____

2. _____

_____

Listen to your teacher read each sentence containing a homophone. Write the homophone on the line.

1. _____

2. _____

3. _____

4. _____

Overview Word Origins

Directions and Sample Answers for Activity Pages

Day 1	See "Model Word Origins" below.
Day 2	Read the title and directions aloud. Invite students to use a dictionary to complete the following word benches: **geology** (*geo* = Greek for "Earth," *logos* = Greek for "logic"): the study of Earth; **mildew** (*mil* = Old English for "honey," *dew* = Old English for "dew"): whitish coating of fungi on plants; **parasol** (*para* = French for "warding off," *sol* = French for "sun"): a small sun umbrella; **transport** (*trans* = Latin for "across," *port* = Latin for "carry"): to carry something from one place to another.
Day 3	Read the title and directions aloud. Invite students to use a dictionary to sort words into four groups: Latin, Greek, Old French/French, and Old English. (Latin: **occur**, **concrete**, **fossil**; Greek: **plankton**, **plasma**, **truck**; Old French/French: **juggle**, **hotel**, **plaque**; Old English: **numb**, **frame**, **warm**. Then have students identify word origins for the words in the list. **tea**–Chinese, **tattoo**–Tahitian, **walleye**–Scandinavian, **damp**–German)
Day 4	Read the title and directions aloud. Invite students to read the words and their origins. Then locate the words in the word search.
Day 5	Read the directions aloud. Allow time for students to complete the first task of identifying origins: **decline**: (Latin): to fall away; **decade** (Greek): ten, **deck** (Dutch): to cover. Next, pronounce the words **fossil**, **damp**, **frame**, and **juggle**, and ask students to write them on the lines. Afterward, meet individually with students. Ask them to read each word on the assessment page. Discuss their results. Use their responses to plan further instruction and review.

Model Word Origins

◆ Hand out the Day 1 activity page. Write **sage**, **hyena**, **television**, **sausage**, **miff**, **ham**, **hamlet**, and **hammock** on the board.

◆ **Say:** *Many English words have their beginnings from other languages. Some of our words come from Greek and Latin, while other words originate from French and German. The study of word origins is called etymology. Understanding a word's etymology helps you read and understand unfamiliar words.*

◆ **Say:** *Look at the word **sage** on the board. This word originates from the Latin word **sapere**, which means "to be wise." In English, **sage** means "a wise person."*

◆ Repeat with **hyena**; **television** (*tele* is Greek for "far off" and *vis* is Latin for "to see"); **sausage** (French: *saucisse*) meat minced and seasoned then enclosed in the intestines of pig or sheep; and **miff** (German: from *muffen*–to sulk) to put into a bad mood.

◆ **Say:** *We also have many words that look similar, but have different origins. Look at **ham**, **hamlet**, and **hammock**. **Ham** and **hamlet** are Old English. **Ham** is meat from a hog's thigh and was originally spelled **hamm** with two **m**'s. **Hamlet** is a village and was originally spelled **ham** with one **m**. **Hammock** comes from the Spanish word **hamaca**, which means "hanging bed."*

Word Origins

sage	(Latin: *sapere*) to be wise
hyena	(Greek: *huaina*) sow-like
television	(Greek: *tele*) far off + (Latin: *vis*) to see
sausage	(French: *saucisse*) seasoned with salt
miff	(German: *muffen*) to offend
ham	(Old English: *hamm*) pigmeat
hamlet	(Old English: *ham*) village or town
hammock	(Spanish: *hamaca*) hanging bed

...ns

...of each word. Then write the definition.

...glish Word	Origin and Meaning and Spelling of Original Word	English Definition
sage		
hyena		
television		
sausage		
miff		
ham		
hamlet		
hammock		

Word Benches

Many English words can be divided into two parts. These words can be analyzed using word benches. Look at the following example:

archaeologist

arkhaios	definition:	logos
Greek for "ancient"	a scientist who studies ancient civilizations	Greek for "reason"

Use a dictionary to complete the following word benches. Share your work with a partner.

geology

mildew

parasol

transport

...ıs Word Sort

...wing words. **Use a dictionary to sort the words into four groups: Latin, Greek,**
...**French, and Old English. Share your work with a partner.**

truck	occur	fossil	frame
juggle	hotel	plankton	plasma
warm	numb	concrete	plaque

Latin	**Greek**	**Old French/ French**	**Old English**

Read the following words. Use a dictionary to determine their word origins. Write the origins on the lines provided.

tea _____

tattoo (on the skin) _____

walleye_____

damp_____

Word Search

Read the words and their origins in the box. Then find each word in the word search.

Old French	Old English	Latin	Greek	Spanish	Arabic
train	aspen	traitor	octopus	bolero	borax
arrest	blood	predict	thermos		

t	r	a	i	t	o	r	k	b	p
h	g	r	f	n	m	g	h	r	c
e	h	r	s	a	s	p	e	n	w
r	t	e	u	d	e	d	q	j	z
m	d	s	p	y	i	f	d	u	x
o	o	t	o	c	b	j	i	x	a
s	o	p	t	r	a	i	n	q	r
e	l	p	c	t	s	v	a	y	o
m	b	u	o	o	r	e	l	o	b

Name _____

Assessment

Use a dictionary to identify the origin and original meaning for each word.

Word	Origin	Original Meaning
decline	_____	_____
decade	_____	_____
deck	_____	_____

Listen to your teacher say each word. Write the word on the line.

1. _____

2. _____

3. _____

4. _____